PENGUIN BOOKS

THE SECOND BOOK
OF INSULTS

Nancy McPhee is an experienced
writer, researcher, and broadcaster.
Married, with three school-aged children, she is an honor graduate of Trin-
ity College, University of Toronto. As
a director, writer, and story editor she
was involved in the halcyon early days
of Canadian live television in Toronto,
specializing in the field of public affairs. As a free-lancer, she has under-
taken writing, research, and editorial
work for a wide variety of Canadian
magazines, publishing houses, busi-
nesses, and government agencies. She is
the author of *The Book of Insults,* also
published by Penguin Books.

For John .. ...

Another curious compilation
of querulous commentaries,
egregious incivilities,
rapacious repartee
and captious criticism,
culled from the calumnies
of the past and present
for the edification of
the mildly malicious.

THE SECOND
BOOK OF

Insults

by Nancy McPhee

PENGUIN BOOKS

Penguin Books Ltd, Harmondsworth,
Middlesex, England
Penguin Books, 625 Madison Avenue,
New York, New York 10022, U.S.A.
Penguin Books Australia Ltd, Ringwood,
Victoria, Australia
Penguin Books Canada Limited, 2801 John Street,
Markham, Ontario, Canada L3R 1B4
Penguin Books (N.Z.) Ltd, 182–190 Wairau Road,
Auckland 10, New Zealand

First published in the United States of America by
St. Martin's Press, Inc., 1981
Published in Penguin Books 1983

LIBRARY OF CONGRESS CATALOGING IN PUBLICATION DATA
Main entry under title:
The Second book of insults.
Includes index.
1. Invective.   I. McPhee, Nancy.   II. Title:
Insults.
PN6231.I65S4   1983   808.88′2   82-22239
ISBN 0 14 00.6474 5

Printed in the United States of America by
R. R. Donnelley & Sons Company, Harrisonburg, Virginia

Illustrated by Graham Pilsworth

ACKNOWLEDGMENTS

The author wishes to thank the following for permission to reprint material included in this book: A&W Publishers, Inc. for extracts from *The Book of Days* by Elizabeth Donaldson and Gerald Donaldson. Abelard-Schuman Ltd. for extracts from *I Wish I'd Said That* by Kenneth Edwards, and for extracts from *I Wish I'd Said That Too!* by Kenneth Edwards. George Allen & Unwin Publishers Ltd. for extracts from *Quote . . . Unquote* by Nigel Rees. Brandt & Brandt Literary Agents, Inc. for extracts from *The Age of Wellington* copyright © 1963 by Leonard Cooper. Cassell Ltd. for extracts from *The Five Hundred Best English Letters*, edited by Frederick Edwin Smith Birkenhead. Citadel Press for extracts from *The Algonquin Wits* by Robert Drennon, published by arrangement with Lyle Stuart Inc. William Collins Sons & Co. Canada Ltd. for an extract from *Colombo's Hollywood* by John Robert Colombo. Delacorte Press for extracts from *Dictionary of Quotations* by Bergen Evans, and for extracts from *The Hater's Handbook* by Joseph Rosner. The *Detroit Free Press* for a comment by Ronald Reagan. Dodd, Mead & Co. for extracts from *The Home Book of Quotations* edited by Burton Stevenson, and for extracts from *The Home Book of Humorous Quotations*, edited by A.K. Adams. E.P. Dutton Publishing Co. Inc. for extracts from *The Fine Art of Political Wit* by Leonard A. Harris. Eyre & Spottiswoode Publishers Ltd. for extracts from *More Invective* by Hugh Kingsmill, and for extracts from *An Anthology of Invective and Abuse* by Hugh Kingsmill. John Stevenson Publisher for extracts from *Insults — A Practical Anthology* by Max Herzberg, published originally by Greystone Press. Harper & Row, Publishers, Inc. for extracts from *A Treasury of Humorous Quotations* by Herbert V. Prochnow, for extracts from *Collections & Recollections I* by G.W.E. Russell, originally published by Harper & Brothers, and for extracts from *The Smith of Smiths* by Hesketh Pearson, originally published by Harper & Brothers. William Heinemann Ltd. A.P. Watt for extracts from *Lives of The Wits* by Hesketh Pearson, for extracts from *The Soul of Wit* by George Rostrevor Hamilton. Hurtig Publishers Ltd. for extracts from *Colombo's Little Book of Canadian Proverbs, Graffiti, Limericks and Other Vital Matters* by John Robert Colombo. Alfred A. Knopf, Inc. for extracts from *A New Dictionary of Quotations* by H.L. Mencken, and for extracts from *The Dictionary of Biographical Quotations* by Richard Kenin & Justin Wintle. Macmillan Publishing Co. Inc. for extracts from *The Last Word* by Louis Kronenberger, and for extracts from *The Second Post* edited by Edward Verall Lucas. Methuen & Co. Ltd. for an extract from *The Gentlest Art*, edited by Edward Verall Lucas, and for extracts from *A Book of Famous Wits* by Walter Copeland Jerrold. Oxford University Press for extracts from *Selected Letters of Sydney Smith,* edited by Nowell C. Smith. Penguin Books Ltd. for extracts from *Penguin Dictionary of Quotations* by J.M. Cohen and M.J. Cohen, published by Allen Lane. G.P. Putnam's Sons for extracts from *The Wit and Wisdom of Sydney Smith* by Sydney Smith. The Warden and Fellows of Nuffield College, Oxford for extracts from *William Cobbett* by James Sambrook. Rutgers University Press for extracts from *William Cobbett: His Thoughts & His Times* copyright © 1966 by John W. Osborne. Charles Scribner's Sons for an extract from *Nineteenth Century English Letters,* edited by Byron Johnson Rees.

Although every effort has been made to ensure that permissions for all material were obtained, those sources not formally acknowledged here will be included in all future editions of this book.

CONTENTS

FOREWORD

Before I published *The Book of Insults, Ancient and Modern* three years ago, I thought I was an eccentric person. There I was, chortling gleefully over a choice piece of invective — an elegant but ill-intentioned eighteenth-century missive, perhaps, or a cuttingly short, sharply barbed sample of malicious wit — while everyone else hungered for the Good, the True and the Beautiful. But the success of *The Book of Insults* and my experience on scores of open-line radio programs have convinced me that I am not alone. There are thousands and thousands of us, all cherishing our own little hordes of bad-natured commentaries, preferring a malicious quip to an uplifting thought, and demanding only that the bad-mouthing be redeemed by wit, grace and style in the use of language. Out of the closet, ye legions of the nasty-minded! It is for you that *The Second Book of Insults* is intended.

Not caring to chew my cabbage twice, I have tried to avoid making this book a carbon copy of its predecessor. I have taken the opportunity to explore a little more fully a number of colorful characters who fascinated me, and have dabbled in two of my favorite forms, the letter and the epitaph. Such famous letters as that of Dr. Johnson to Lord Chesterfield and of Junius to the Duke of Grafton were, of course, featured in the first book, and are not repeated here. Once again I have interpreted "insult" as widely as possible, and the quotations range from bitter diatribe to irreverent doggerel and mild incivility. Their common feature is that I enjoyed them.

I owe a debt of gratitude to many people, of whom only a few can be named here. To Dr. Ian Storey of Trent University, for access to an unpublished PhD thesis; to my boss, Rick Frost of the Region of Peel, for his forbearance and occasionally blind eye; to Allan Stormont and Patrick Crean, of Ganton Gate Books for their patience and understanding; and to my editor, Charlotte Weiss, for her good humor, professionalism and wise advice, which I did not always heed. My deepest thanks must go to my long-suffering family: to my children, Peter, Patrick and Andrea, for always chuckling in the right places and for rising cheerfully above a relentless diet of hamburgers and tomato soup; and above all to John, my first husband, for his research and editorial advice, for countless middle-of-the-night cigarettes and cups of tea, and for his unfailing encouragement and support over many years.

A number of people read portions of the manuscript in draft form and made comments and suggestions. It goes without saying that the book's many deficiencies are entirely their fault, while any virtues it may possess are all my own.

N.G.M.

1981

CHAPTER ONE

Forgive Thine Enemies

Always forgive your enemies — but never forget their names.
Robert F. Kennedy (1925-1968)

ROBERT KENNEDY

The French, of course, have a word for it — *l'esprit de l'escalier*. Staircase wit — the perfect retort that comes on the way downstairs, long after it would have been useful. Most of us are staircase wits, and we admire all the more those ready spirits who are poised with a verbal stiletto — who jab, prod or run through an opponent as we ourselves can never do.

The effective insult takes many forms. It may be oral and spontaneous, a happy thought striking at just the right moment. Or it may be polished and literary, the careful product of long and malicious effort. At its best it combines an aptness to its subject with a flair for words that leaves even the victim applauding. Pure invective — the piling up of real or fancied indignation into a Niagara of abuse — has its place, and so, too, does the pure wisecrack, although this last must contain at least a kernel of truth to have a staying power beyond the moment. Incivilities, far more than kind words, are revealing: they can tell as much about the perpetrator as his victim.

The creator of an inspired remark surely performs a service to mankind. Consider, for instance, the total picture of personality conjured up by this comment on a notoriously rotund and rumpled journalist:

A one-man slum.

Anonymous on Heywood Broun

or the pinch-faced image of a somewhat less than memorable U.S. president:

A victim of the use of water as a beverage.

Sam Houston (1793-1863) on James K. Polk

or on the nasal impact of a celebrated novelist:

An animated adenoid.

Anonymous on Ford Madox Ford

The creator of that novel beloved by teenagers, *The Catcher in the Rye,* was skewered by a contemporary who has himself been the target of countless insults:

The greatest mind ever to stay in prep school.
> Norman Mailer (b. 1923) on J. D. Salinger

And, of course, media personalities are always an easy mark:

A legend in his own lunchtime.
> Christopher Wordsworth on
> journalist Clifford Makins

He rose without a trace.
> Kitty Muggeridge on TV interviewer David Frost

Self-revelation can take place either consciously or unconsciously:

I'm as pure as driven slush.
> Tallulah Bankhead (1903-1968) on herself

I liked your opera. I think I will set it to music.
> Ludwig van Beethoven (1770-
> 1827) to a fellow composer

Cool sophistication is at the heart of this icy insult:

He has the heart of a cucumber fried in snow.
> Ninon de Lenclos (1620-1705) on
> the marquis de Sévigné

but a less delicate comparison also gets the message across:

A lamentably successful cross between a fox and a hog.
> James G. Blaine (1830-1893) on
> Benjamin F. Butler

The most successful creative incivility draws a complete and damning picture in a few strokes:

> *He is every other inch a gentleman.*
>
> Noel Coward (1899-1973) on an
> anonymous novelist

> *He has a face like a wedding cake left out in the rain.*
>
> Anonymous on W. H. Auden

> *The King blew his nose twice, and wiped the royal perspiration repeatedly from a face which is probably the largest uncivilized spot in England.*
>
> Oliver Wendell Holmes (1809-1904) on William IV

although a seemingly gentle verbal twist can also be used to telling effect:

> *There goes Jim Fisk, with his hands in his own pockets for a change.*
>
> Anonymous on financier James Fisk

> *Dr. Donne's verses are like the Peace of God, for they pass all understanding.*
>
> James I (1566-1625) on John Donne

A skeptical female demolished a well-known writer's spurious claims to amorous adventure with one deft masterstroke:

> *Some people kiss and tell. George Moore told but did not kiss.*
>
> Susan Mitchell on George Moore

while an Oxford don, suave and sophisticated, strove for the elegant approach:

*What time he can spare from the adornment of his person he
devotes to the neglect of his duties.*
                              Benjamin Jowett (1817-1893) on
                              an undergraduate

and a jovial clergyman put down a self-satisfied friend with ego-
pricking finality:

*I am just going to pray for you at St. Paul's, but with no very
lively hope of success.*
                              Sydney Smith (1771-1845) to Monckton Milnes

And then there is the cryptic remark, espoused by those who
must, surely, know what they mean:

*A village explainer, excellent if you were a village, but if you
were not, not.*
                              Gertrude Stein (1874-1946) on
                              Ezra Pound

The fine art of repartee, the use of the pointed put-down, has
always been cherished. One account records the deflation of a
seventeenth-century actress who was playing a male role:

*This agreable Actress in the Part of Sir Harry coming into the
Greenroom said pleasantly,* In my Conscience, I believe half
the Men in the House take me for one of their own Sex.
Another Actress reply'd, It may be so, but in my Conscience!
the other half can convince them to the Contrary.
                              William Rufus Chetwood
                              (d. 1766) on actress Peg
                              Woffington

The quick retort was a favorite sport even in ancient Greece:

DEMOSTHENES: *The Athenians will kill you some day when they are in a rage.*
PHOCION: *And you, when they are in their senses.*

The witty Bernard Shaw was seldom caught with his defenses down. The gaunt playwright was speaking with a portly newspaper tycoon:

LORD NORTHCLIFFE: *The trouble with you, Shaw, is that you look as if there were a famine in the land.*
SHAW: *The trouble with you, Northcliffe, is that you look as if you were the cause of it.*

When Shaw prepared to take an opening-night bow at one of his plays, a voice from the balcony cried "Boo!"

My friend, I quite agree with you. But what are we two against so many?

Bernard Shaw (1856-1950)

Horatio Bottomley was an arch-charlatan who engaged in a number of dubious financial projects and at last received his just reward. A friend visited Horatio in prison, where he found him stitching mailbags:

VISITOR: *Ah, Bottomley — sewing?*
BOTTOMLEY: *No — reaping.*

Horatio Bottomley (1860-1933)

And then there is this account, possibly even true, of royal weariness with mind-numbing conversation:

OFFICIAL: *And how was your flight, Sir?*
DUKE: *Have you ever flown?*

OFFICIAL: *Oh, yes, Sir, many times.*

DUKE: *Well, it was like that.*

H.R.H. the duke of Edinburgh (b. 1921)

The great Dr. Johnson was afflicted by many hangers-on who tried their best to impress him. One young man lamented the fact that he had now "lost all his Greek":

I believe it happened at the same time, Sir, that I lost all my large estate in Yorkshire.

Samuel Johnson (1709-1784)

One famous and benign father took advantage of an opening that many a parent would welcome:

TOM SHERIDAN: *I think, father, that many men who are called great patriots in the House of Commons are really great humbugs. For my own part, when I get into Parliament, I will pledge myself to no party, but write upon my forehead in legible characters, "To Be Let".*

R. B. SHERIDAN: *And under it, Tom, write "Unfurnished".*

Richard Brinsley Sheridan (1751-1816)

Political debate, of course, lends itself to a ready mind:

LORD CHATHAM: *If I cannot speak standing, I will speak sitting; and if I cannot speak sitting I will speak lying.*

LORD NORTH: *Which he will do in whatever position he speaks.*

Lord North (1732-1792)

VOTER: *Mr. Fox, I admire your head, but damn your heart.*

FOX: *Sir, I admire your candour, but damn your manners.*

Charles James Fox (1749-1806)

VOTER: *You little pipsqueak, I could swallow you in one bite.*

DOUGLAS: *And if you did, my friend, you'd have more brains in your belly than you have in your head.*

Former premier of Saskatchewan
Tommy Douglas (b. 1904)

The law courts provide another useful venue for practicing the art of repartee. One sharp-minded judge was faced with a hesitant and stammering young advocate:

BARRISTER: *The unfortunate client — er — on whose behalf I appear — my unfortunate client —*
ELLENBOROUGH: *You may go on, sir. So far the court is with you.*

Lord Ellenborough (1750-1818)

The silver-tongued Joseph Choate was arguing in a Long Island courtroom:

LAWYER: *Gentlemen, I sincerely hope your decision will not be influenced by the Chesterfieldian urbanity of my opponent.*
CHOATE: *Gentlemen, I am sure you will not be influenced, either, by the Westchesterfieldian suburbanity of my opponent.*

Joseph H. Choate (1832-1917)

The great F. E. Smith, later Lord Birkenhead, was pleading a case before a muddle-headed judge. Seeing His Lordship's confusion, Smith produced a concise and masterly summary of the evidence. It did not help:

JUDGE: *I am sorry, Mr. Smith, but I am none the wiser.*
SMITH: *No, my Lord. But you are better informed.*

F. E. Smith (1872-1930)

British Prime Minister Disraeli attended a public dinner where the meal, served from a distant kitchen, was stone cold. As he sipped his champagne after dinner, he was heard to murmur:

visit to Hollywood she was introduced to femme fatale Jean Harlow, who asked her about the pronunciation of her name:

No, the t *is silent — as in Harlow.*

Margot Asquith (1864-1945)

MARGOT
ASQUITH

Her other sallies tended to make the faint-hearted cringe:

He could not see a belt without hitting below it.

On David Lloyd George

Sir Stafford has a brilliant mind until it is made up.

On Sir Stafford Cripps

Very clever, but his brains go to his head.

On F. E. Smith

The trouble with Lord Birkenhead is that he is so un-Christlike.
On F. E. Smith

His modesty amounts to a deformity.
On her husband, Herbert Asquith

She's as tough as an ox. She'll be turned into Bovril when she dies.
Margot Asquith (1864-1945)

Not everyone appreciated Lady Asquith. Although it was denied, it was generally assumed that a widely circulated poem was composed in her honor:

The haggard cheek, the hungering eye,
The poisoned words that wildly fly,
The famished face, the fevered hand, —
Who slights the worthiest in the land,
Sneers at the just, contemns the brave,
And blackens goodness in its grave . . . .
Malignant-lipped, unkind, unsweet;
Past all example indiscreet.
Who half makes love to you today,
Tomorrow gives her guest away.
William Watson

It was left to Dorothy Parker to have the last word—

The affair between Margot Asquith and Margot Asquith will live as one of the prettiest love stories in all literature.
Dorothy Parker (1893-1967)

Another celebrated harridan was the daughter of President Teddy Roosevelt. "Princess Alice" grew up to be a sharp-tongued lady:

He looks as if he had been weaned on a pickle.
On Calvin Coolidge

The little man on the wedding cake.
On Thomas E. Dewey

One-third Eleanor and two-thirds mush.
On Franklin D. Roosevelt

Eleanor is a Trojan mare.
On Eleanor Roosevelt

Alice Roosevelt Longworth (1893-1967)

and legend had it that her basic philosophy of life was embroidered on a cushion in her drawing room:

If you can't say anything good about somebody, sit right down here beside me.
Alice Roosevelt Longworth (1893-1967)

Yet another crotchety wit, this time a male, was W. S. Gilbert, the verbal half of the sparkling musical team. Neither Gilbert nor his partner thought much of the other:

He is like a man who sits on a stove and then complains that his backside is burning.
Sir William Schwenck Gilbert (1836-1911) on Sir Arthur Sullivan

Another week's rehearsal with WSG & I should have gone raving mad. I had already ordered some straw for my hair.
Sir Arthur Sullivan (1842-1900)
on Sir William Schwenck Gilbert

Sullivan's frustration with rehearsals was justified. Gilbert was renowned as a martinet who would permit no tampering:

GILBERT & SULLIVAN

ACTOR: *Look here, sir, I will not be bullied! I know my lines.*
GILBERT: *That may be, but you don't know mine.*

Tact with actors was completely out of Gilbert's line. To the perspiring star of a first-night production, he remarked:

Your skin has been acting at any rate.
                    To Sir Herbert Beerbohm Tree

And when a prima donna of the day sat down heavily, managing to miss the chair:

Very good, very good. I always thought you would make an impression on the stage one day.
                    To Henrietta Hodson

As the lyrics to his comic operas attest, Gilbert could seldom resist a play on words. Asked by a patently unmusical woman whether Bach was still composing:

No, madam; he's decomposing.

On Johann Sebastian Bach

Gilbert had no great love for the clergy, and one day was appalled to find himself in a room full of clerical collars:

I feel like a lion in a den of Daniels.

When a theater manager praised to the skies an actress with whom he had a rather more than fraternal relationship:

That fellow is blowing his own strumpet.

Perhaps Gilbert's opinion of his fellow man is best summed up by his comment on an old friend:

No one can have a higher opinion of him than I have — and I think he is a dirty little beast.

Sir William Schwenck Gilbert (1836-1911)

The great verbal sallies — or at least those we hear about — are usually directed against politicians, writers, artists — those very much in the public eye. But all sorts and conditions have been the targets of boos and catcalls. Military leaders have frequently irritated their friends and allies:

The greatest cross I have to bear is the Cross of Lorraine.

Winston Churchill (1874-1965)
on Charles de Gaulle

An improbable creature, like a human giraffe, sniffing down his nostrils at mortals beneath his gaze.

Richard Wilson, Lord Moran (b. 1924) on Charles de Gaulle

and when they are public heroes, they can be difficult to endure:

In defeat unbeatable, in victory unbearable.
Winston Churchill (1874-1965)
on Bernard L. Montgomery

There is nothing new in this. In the United States, veteran army men after the Civil War were incensed when Adolphus Greely was made a general. He had spent much time as an Arctic explorer, suffering terrible hardships, but had little experience with troops:

He never commanded more than ten men in his life — and he ate three of them.
General Weston on Adolphus W. Greely

In another field, the pretensions of scholars and men of learning have often been open to ridicule. A famous master of Balliol College at Oxford was the victim of a popular parody:

First come I; my name is Jowett.
There's no knowledge but I know it.
I am Master of this College:
And what I don't know isn't knowledge.
H. C. Beeching (1859-1919) on Benjamin Jowett

and another, more recent, "engaged scholar" found his antiwar activities disapproved of:

If I were the Prince of Peace I should choose a less provocative ambassador.
A. E. Housman (1859-1936) on Bertrand Russell

Even distinguished scientists have found that their discoveries are not always appreciated:

Sir Humphrey Davy
Abominated gravy.
He lived in the odium
Of having discovered sodium.

E. C. Bentley (1875-1956) on Humphrey Davy

For some reason, symphony conductors have frequently been noted for the sharp points on their batons. Sir Thomas Beecham's pithy remarks were famous — to a tone-deaf choir:

If you will make a point of singing "All we, like sheep, have gone astray" with a little less satisfaction, we shall meet the aesthetical as well as the theological requirements.

Sir Thomas Beecham (1879-1961)

and, with barely muted sarcasm, on the occasion of his seventieth birthday. As the messages of congratulations were read, he muttered:

What, nothing from Mozart?

Sir Thomas Beecham (1879-1961)

Mozart would have had a hard time matching his ego:

I am not the greatest conductor in this country. On the other hand I'm better than any damned foreigner.

Sir Thomas Beecham (1879-1961)

Beecham was not really all that impressed with his contemporaries and rivals:

A glorified bandmaster!

Sir Thomas Beecham (1879-1961) on Arturo Toscanini

and they tended to return the compliment:

> *He conducted like a dancing dervish.*
> Sir John Barbirolli (1899-1970)
> on Sir Thomas Beecham

Barbirolli himself inspired no mean awe amongst his players. One of these, paying a parking fine, explained:

> *I prefer to face the wrath of the police rather than the wrath of Sir John Barbirolli.*
> Anonymous orchestra member
> on Sir John Barbirolli

Meanwhile, across the pond, the ferocious New York maestro had his own threats to keep the musicians in line:

> *After I die, I shall return to earth as a gatekeeper of a bordello and I won't let any of you — not a one of you — enter.*
> Arturo Toscanini (1867-1957)

The world of popular entertainment is not so different from the world of classical music. A sardonic director had the right approach to the making of films:

> *I deny that I said that actors are like cattle. I said they should be treated like cattle.*
> Alfred Hitchcock (1899-1980)

Actors' lives in Hollywood do tend to be sheeplike. Careers are dominated by powerful but ungrammatical columnists:

> *She never avoids phrases like "the reason is because" unless it is impossible not to do so, and she likes her infinitives split.*
> Anonymous on Louella Parsons

and by impresarios who like to repeat their last big hit:

> *Cecil B. de Mille,*
> *Rather against his will,*
> *Was persuaded to leave Moses*
> *Out of "The Wars of the Roses".*
>
> Nicholas Bentley (b. 1907) on C. B. de Mille

Even the most mythical of popular entertainers has suffered the slings and arrows of the unappreciative critic:

> *Mr. Presley has no discernable singing ability. His specialty is rhythm songs which he renders in an undistinguished whine; his phrasing, if it can be called that, consists of the stereotyped variations that go with a beginner's aria in a bathtub. For the ear he is an unutterable bore . . . . He is a rock-and-roll variation of one of the most standard acts in show business: the virtuoso of the hootchy-kootchy.*
>
> Jack Gould (b. 1917) on Elvis Presley

Some connoisseurs feel that contemporary invective is just not up to scratch. And while it is true that there is nothing particularly memorable, wise, witty or profound in the standard Hollywood wisecrack, the denizens of tinsel town have produced some good lines —

> *A day away from Tallulah Bankhead is like a month in the country.*
>
> Anonymous on Tallulah Bankhead

> *When Jack Benny plays the violin, it sounds as if the strings are still back in the cat.*
>
> Fred Allen (1894-1956) on Jack Benny

I never forget a face — but in your case I'll make an exception.

I've had a wonderful evening, but this wasn't it.

Groucho Marx (1890-1977)

I am free of all prejudice. I hate everyone equally.

I always keep a supply of stimulant handy in case I see a snake — which I also keep handy.

W. C. Fields (1880-1946)

I don't have to look up my family tree, because I know that I'm the sap.

Fred Allen (1894-1956) on himself

And, on one occasion at least, a great line:

Please accept my resignation. I don't want to belong to any club that will accept me as a member.

Groucho Marx (1890-1977)

More even than in the entertainment world, waspishness and backbiting are traditional in literary circles, and the tradition goes back a surprisingly long way. A thirteenth-century Italian poet was victimized by subsequent nitpickers:

A Methodist parson in Bedlam.

Horace Walpole (1717-1797) on Dante

A hyena that wrote poetry in tombs.

Friedrich Nietzsche (1844-1900) on Dante

In the volatile world of Elizabethan England, writers were particularly prone to voice delicate criticisms of one another's work:

He can raile (what mad Bedlam cannot raile?) but the favour of his railing, is grosely fell, and smelleth noysomly of the pumps, or a nastier thing.... His jestes [are] but the dregges of common scurrilitie... like old pickle herring: his lustiest verdure, but rank ordure, not be named in Civilitie, or Rhetorique.

> Gabriel Harvey (1545-1630) on Thomas Nashe

It seems that the Elizabethans set an example that later writers have been loath to abandon:

He was an instance that a complete genius and a complete rogue can be formed before a man is of age.

> Horace Walpole (1717-1797) on
> Thomas Chatterton

Bulwer-Lytton I detest. He is the very pimple of the age's humbug.

> Nathaniel Hawthorne (1804-1864) on Edward Bulwer-Lytton

He never wrote an invitation to dinner without an eye to posterity.

> Benjamin Disraeli (1804-1881) on Edward Bulwer-Lytton

On Waterloo's ensanguined plain
Lie tens of thousands of the slain;
But none, by sabre or by shot,
Fell half so flat as Walter Scott.

> Thomas, Lord Erskine (1750-1823) on Sir Walter Scott's *The Field of Waterloo*

Some authors seem naturally to draw fire around their heads. Bernard Shaw delighted in being a gadfly, but his contemporaries showed no hesitation in prodding back:

George Too Shaw To Be Good.

> Dylan Thomas (1914-1953)

That noisiest of old cocks.
Wyndham Lewis (1884-1957)

Too much gas-bag.
D. H. Lawrence (1885-1930) on Bernard Shaw

Some of them detected a streak of puritanism beneath Shaw's thick skin:

His brain is a half-inch layer of champagne poured over a bucket of Methodist near-beer.
Benjamin de Casseres

The first man to have cut a swathe through the theatre and left it strewn with virgins.
Frank Harris (1856-1931) on Bernard Shaw

but the most common complaint was simply that he talked too much:

When you were quite a little boy somebody ought to have said "hush" just once.
Mrs. Patrick Campbell (1865-1940) to Bernard Shaw

Relationships between writers have tended to combine friendship, envy, and enmity in equal portions. Few have been anxious to restrain the critical spirit:

He is conscious of being decrepit and forgetful, but not of being a bore.
Evelyn Waugh (1903-1966) on Hilaire Belloc

He would not blow his nose without moralising on conditions in the handkerchief industry.
Cyril Connolly (1903-1975) on
George Orwell

Chesterton is like a vile scum on a pond. . . . All his slop!
Ezra Pound (1895-1972) on G. K.
Chesterton

Things could get particularly sticky when husband and wife both followed a literary bent:

Mr. Fitzgerald — I believe that is how he spells his name — seems to believe that plagiarism begins at home.
Zelda Fitzgerald (1900-1957) on husband, F. Scott Fitzgerald

and in close-knit literary circles, where everyone knew and gossiped about everyone else, almost nothing was beyond the pale. Inevitably, some members came in for special attention — Arnold Bennett, whose fascination with money was a byword:

Bennett — sort of pig in clover.
D. H. Lawrence (1885-1930)

Nickel cash-register Bennett.
Ezra Pound (1895-1972)

The Hitler of the book racket.
Wyndham Lewis (1884-1957) on Arnold Bennett

the trendy Max Beerbohm:

He has the most remarkable and seductive genius — and I should say about the smallest in the world.
Lytton Strachey (1880-1932)

He is a shallow, affected, self-conscious fribble.
Vita Sackville-West

Tell me, when you are alone with Max, does he take off his face and reveal his mask?
Oscar Wilde (1854-1900) on Max Beerbohm

and the quixotic Gertrude Stein, whose elusive prose brought out the metaphor in others:

What an old covered-wagon she is!
                                    F. Scott Fitzgerald (1896-1940)

Gertrude Stein's prose is a cold, black suet-pudding. We can represent it as a cold suet-roll of fabulously reptilian length. Cut it at any point, it is . . . the same heavy, sticky, opaque mass all through, and all along.
                        Wyndham Lewis (1884-1957) on Gertrude Stein

George Moore — he who told without kissing — was a favorite victim of his comrades:

George Moore is always conducting his education in public.
                                    Oscar Wilde (1854-1900)

That old pink petulant walrus.
                                    Henry Channon

He leads his readers to the latrine and locks them in.
                        Oscar Wilde (1854-1900) on George Moore

Moore was quite capable of fighting back, when he cared to:

Oscar Wilde's talent seems to me essentially rootless, something growing in a glass in a little water.
                                    George Moore (1852-1933) on
                                    Oscar Wilde

and in his autobiography, pretentiously titled *Ave Atque Vale*, he gave a verbal drubbing to one of his former professors in Dublin. The old Latin scholar sniffed scornfully:

Moore is one of those folks who think that "Atque" was a Roman centurion.
Robert Yelverton Tyrrell (1844-1914) on George Moore

Novelist Ford Madox Ford, the "animated adenoid," was another favorite target. For his part, he enjoyed the sport himself:

Conrad spent a day finding the mot juste, *and then killed it.*
Ford Madox Ford (1873-1939) on
Joseph Conrad

but he certainly got as good as he gave:

Master, mammoth mumbler.
Robert Lowell (1917-1977)

His mind was like a Roquefort cheese, so ripe that it was palpably falling to pieces.
Van Wyck Brooks (1886-1963)

Freud Madox Fraud.
Osbert Sitwell (1892-1969) on Ford Madox Ford

Close little literary circles are a veritable hive of unfriendly gossip:

Pale, marmoreal Eliot was there last week, like a chapped office boy on a high stool, with a cold in his head.
Virginia Woolf (1882-1941) on T. S. Eliot

All raw, uncooked, protesting.
Virginia Woolf (1882-1941) on
Aldous Huxley

DAME
EDITH
SITWELL

I thought nothing *of her writing. I considered her a "beautiful little knitter."*

Edith Sitwell (1887-1964) on Virginia Woolf

Mr. Lawrence looked like a plaster gnome on a stone toadstool in some suburban garden.... He looked as if he had just returned from spending an uncomfortable night in a very dark cave.

Edith Sitwell (1887-1964) on D. H. Lawrence

but occasionally one of the group is singled out for special attention:

I do not think I have ever seen a nastier-looking man. . . . Under the black hat, when I had first seen them, the eyes had been those of an unsuccessful rapist.
                        Ernest Hemingway (1899-1961)
                        on Wyndham Lewis

A buffalo in wolf's clothing.
                        Robert Ross on Wyndham Lewis

Mr. Lewis's pictures appeared . . . to have been painted by a mailed fist in a cotton glove.
                        Edith Sitwell (1887-1964) on Wyndham Lewis

Edith . . . is a bad loser. When worsted in argument, she throws Queensbury Rules to the winds. She once called me Percy.
                        Percy Wyndham Lewis (1884-
                        1957) on Edith Sitwell

It took unfeeling outsiders, however, to put the discussion into perspective:

The Sitwells belong to the history of publicity rather than of poetry.
                        F. R. Leavis (1895-1978)

So you've been reviewing Edith Sitwell's latest piece of virgin dung, have you? Isn't she a poisonous thing of a woman, lying, concealing, flipping, plagiarising, misquoting, and being as clever a crooked literary publicist as ever.
                        Dylan Thomas (1914-1953) on Edith Sitwell

Even more than writers, politicians expect, and get, a constant barrage of public criticism. Powerful presidents are not immune. Teddy Roosevelt had many a run-in with the financial powers-that-be, and he was hated in the stock exchanges. When he departed on a well-publicized safari to Africa, a sign appeared on the New York trading floor:

Wall Street Expects Every Lion To Do Its Duty.
Anonymous

Roosevelt was a fanatic about the simplification of English spelling — an enthusiasm which permitted one New York paper to applaud his retirement from office with a parting shot:

THRU!
Anonymous on Theodore Roosevelt

Other U.S. presidents have fielded a variety of caustic comments:

To nominate Grover Cleveland would be to march through a slaughterhouse into an open grave.
Henry Watterson on Grover Cleveland

He had a bungalow mind.
Woodrow Wilson (1856-1924) on Warren G. Harding

A fat Coolidge.
H. L. Mencken (1880-1956) on Herbert Hoover

A chameleon on plaid.
Herbert Hoover (1874-1964) on Franklin D. Roosevelt

The croon of croons.
H. L. Mencken (1880-1956) on Franklin D. Roosevelt

He looks like the guy in a science fiction movie who is the first to see the Creature.
David Frye on Gerald Ford

Every prospective U.S. president has to endure an arduous election campaign, but some don't appear to mind losing favor with at least part of the public:

> *A hippie is someone who looks like Tarzan, walks like Jane and smells like Cheeta.*
>
> Ronald Reagan (b. 1911) on losing the hippie vote

Abraham Lincoln's presidential opponent had to overcome apparently insuperable difficulties:

> *Douglas never can be president, Sir. No, Sir; Douglas never can be president, Sir. His legs are too short, Sir. His coat, like a cow's tail, hangs too near the ground, Sir.*
>
> Thomas Hart Benton (1782-1858)
> on Stephen A. Douglas

but in any case, Lincoln appeared to have his measure:

> *I did keep a grocery, and I did sell cotton, candles and cigars, and sometimes whiskey; but I remember in those days Mr. Douglas was one of my best customers. Many a time have I stood on one side of the counter and sold whiskey to Mr. Douglas on the other side, but the difference between us now is this: I have left my side of the counter, but Mr. Douglas still sticks to his as tenaciously as ever.*
>
> Abraham Lincoln (1809-1865) on
> Stephen A. Douglas

Not just presidents, but royal princes are on the receiving end of criticism. It comes hard, however, from one's nearest and dearest:

> *His intellect is no more use than a pistol packed in the bottom of a trunk if one were attacked in the robber-infested Apennines.*
>
> Prince Albert (1819-1861) on his son, later Edward VII

Even minor and long-forgotten American politicians have had to face the hoots and gibes of their contemporaries:

Damn John Jay! Damn every one that won't damn John Jay! Damn every one that won't put lights in his windows and sit up all night damning John Jay!!!

Anonymous on John Jay, 1794

Mr. Ames's friends treated his memory as they did his body.

John Quincy Adams (1767-1848)
on Fisher Ames

A becurled and perfumed grandee gazed at by the gallery-gapers.

James G. Blaine (1830-1893) on Roscoe Conkling

Wallowing in corruption like a rhinoceros in an African pool.

E. L. Godkin (1831-1902) on James G. Blaine

No man in our annals has filled so large a space and left it so empty.

Charles Edward Russell on James G. Blaine

In Great Britain, things were no better. Complain, complain, complain:

He was oppressed by metaphor, dislocated by parentheses, and debilitated by amplification.

Samuel Parr (1747-1825) on a speech by Edmund Burke

His temper naturally morose, has become licentiously peevish. Crossed in his Cabinet, he insults the House of Lords, and plagues the most eminent of his colleagues with the crabbed malice of a maundering witch.

Benjamin Disraeli (1804-1881)
on the earl of Aberdeen

Dangerous as an enemy, untrustworthy as a friend, but fatal as a colleague.

Sir Hercules Robinson on Joseph Chamberlain

He has the mind and manners of a clothes brush.

Harold Nicholson (1886-1968) on Austen Chamberlain

D. is a very weak-minded fellow I am afraid, and, like the feather pillow, bears the marks of the last person who has sat on him! I hear he is called in London "genial Judas"!

General Douglas Haig (1861-1928) on the 17th earl of Derby

Black and wicked and with only a nodding acquaintance with the truth.

Lady Cunard on Herbert Asquith

His fame endures; we shall not forget
The name of Baldwin until we're out of debt.

Kensal Green on Stanley Baldwin

Every time Mr. Macmillan comes back from abroad Mr. Butler goes to the airport and grips him warmly by the throat.

Harold Wilson (b. 1916) on Harold Macmillan and R.A.B. Butler

In the face of all this political Billingsgate, one has only two options — to follow the dictates of a master political strategist:

Never complain. Never explain. Get even.

Robert F. Kennedy (1925-1968)

or, like Matthew Arnold, to take refuge in philosophy:

When Abraham Lincoln was murdered
The one thing that interested Matthew Arnold

Was that the assassin shouted in Latin
As he leaped from the stage.
This convinced Matthew
There was still hope for America.

Christopher Morley (1890-1957)

You slawzy poodle, you tike,
You crapulous puddering pipsqueak!

Christopher Fry (b. 1907) *The
Lady's Not for Burning*

Get out, you blazing ass!
Gabble o' the goose. Don't bugaboo-baby me!

C. S. Calverley (1831-1884) *The
Cock and the Bull*

Shut your fat gob, you nasty little pile of wombat's do's!
Monty Python's Flying Circus, "A Bad Conversation with the Queen"

CHAPTER TWO

The Poisoned Pen

TALLEYRAND

Long before that monument to inefficiency, the modern post office, became the institution everybody loves to hate, the letter had established itself as the perfect vehicle for the expression of malicious wit. What better opportunity to polish a well-turned phrase while preserving the appearance of spontaneity, to jab with a pointed sentence or cascade paragraphs of scorn on one's hapless victim? And for us, the unintended readers of this uncivil correspondence, there is the guilty enjoyment of the voyeur — as we intrude on the privacy and eavesdrop on the less than worthy thoughts of others.

The letter's effectiveness as a personal weapon has undoubtedly declined since the formidable days of Junius and Dr. Johnson. Their lengthy and studied insolence is no longer in vogue. Today, our greatest admiration is reserved for those who can condense their wit into a few brief phrases. A classic, if apocryphal, example is this plea from an English schoolboy to his father:

S.O.S. L.S.D. R.S.V.P.

Anonymous

It is perhaps necessary, in a decimal age, to add that the second set of letters refers to pounds, shillings and pence.

The puckish wit of the French statesman Talleyrand is demonstrated in this pair of letters sent, with the briefest of intervals, to a beautiful widow; the first on the death of her husband:

Hélas, madame!

the second on her remarriage:

Ho! ho! madame!

Charles Maurice de Talleyrand-Périgord (1754-1838)

When a clergyman serving under a 19th-century English bishop requested a leave of absence to travel to the Holy Land, the good shepherd's reply went directly to the point:

> Dear Sir:
> Go to Jericho.
>   Yours,
>   A.W.R.

Anthony William Thorold (1825-1895)

Bernard Shaw once achieved an unaccustomed brevity in responding to a collector of social scalps. Receiving a card with the inscription:

> Lady ——— will be at home on Thursday between four and six o'clock.

Shaw returned the invitation with the handwritten notation:

> Mr. Bernard Shaw likewise.

Bernard Shaw (1856-1950)

The writer Hilaire Belloc was at one time engaged by the London *Morning Post,* where he frustrated his employers by his infrequent appearances and his proprietary air. One can only picture the scene which led to this little cry of pent-up fury from his editor:

March 23, 1909

> Dear Belloc,
> I owe you an apology for the way I shouted at you this afternoon; but please don't, on your rare and unexpected visits to the office (about which I shall say more on another occasion) stand in my door and wag a finger at me when I am engaged on private and difficult business.
>   Yours,
>   F.W.

Fabian Ware (1869-1949) to Hilaire Belloc

Paternal pride is a noble feeling. But the father of a shockingly irreverent satirist was willing to put it to one side to spare his own feelings:

> *May 29, 1872*
> *Dear Sam,*
> *I shall take your advice and not read your book. It would probably pain me and not benefit you.*
> > *Your affectionate father,*
> > T. BUTLER
>
> Canon T. Butler to Samuel Butler

Unrequested and unwanted gifts always create the problem of acknowledgment:

> *Many thanks for your book; I shall lose no time in reading it.*
> Benjamin Disraeli (1804-1881)

or the well-meaning friend who unloads her latest bargain —

> *I thank you for the snip of cloth, commonly called a pattern. At present I have two coats and but one back. If at any time hereafter I should find myself possessed of fewer coats and more backs, it will be of use to me.*
> William Cowper (1731-1800); letter to Lady Hesketh

Other unsolicited presentations seem to cry out for a clever response. A bottle of fruit, for instance, preserved in brandy:

> DEAR AUNT,
> *A thousand thanks for your kind gift. I appreciate the cherries immensely, not so much for themselves as for the spirit in which they are sent.*
> > Anonymous

or the bounties of summer sent to a not ungrateful but ironical canon:

What is real piety? What is true attachment to the Church? How are these fine feelings best evinced? The answer is plain: by sending strawberries to a clergyman. Many thanks.
                                    Sydney Smith (1771-1845)

The preservation of sanity and temper from time to time demands the short, sharp retort. During one school crisis the head of Haileybury College was inundated with well-meaning advice from parents and friends. In self-defense he printed up a postcard — an idea that anyone obliged to court public opinion today might well duplicate:

DEAR SIR,
I am obliged by your opinions, and retain my own.
                                    Anonymous

But then, friendship is a fragile thing at best. Did it survive, one wonders, this little interchange between a political candidate and his near neighbor?

                                    February 28, 1820

MY DEAR SIR,
In times like the present, it is impossible to allow private feelings to take the place of a public sense of duty. I think your conduct as dangerous in Parliament as it is in your own county. Were you my own brother, therefore, I could not give you my support.
        THOMAS LIDDELL

MY DEAR SIR THOMAS,
In answer to your letter, I beg to say that I feel gratitude for your frankness, compassion for your fears, little dread of your opposition, and no want of your support. — I am, etc.,
        J. G. LAMBTON

Certainly there was a relish in the twist with which a Philadelphia kite-flyer put an end to an even longer friendship:

> You are a member of Parliament, and one of that majority which has doomed my country to destruction. — You have begun to burn our towns, and murder our people. — Look upon your hands! They are stained with the blood of your relations! — You and I were long friends: — You are now my enemy, — and I am
> Yours
> B. FRANKLIN

Benjamin Franklin (1706-1790);
letter to William Strahan

Both friendships and family ties are often strained by finances, and when money-talk finds its way into personal letters acrimony is almost sure to ensue. Long before he declined to read his son's book, Canon Butler had expressed the exact worth of young Sam's talents:

> *May 9, 1859*
> Dear Sam:
> If you choose to act in utter contradiction of our judgment and wishes, and that before having acquired the slightest knowledge of your powers which I see you overrate in other points, you can of course act as you like. But I think it right to tell you that not one sixpence will you receive from me after your Michaelmas payment till you come to your senses. . . .

Canon T. Butler to Samuel Butler

Letters appealing for money run the risk of being unsympathetically received. The samaritan who requested a donation to pay off the mortgage of the Duke Street Chapel got more than he bargained for:

BRANTWOOD, *19th May, 1886*

SIR,

I am scornfully amused at your appeal to me, of all people in the world the precisely least likely to give you a farthing! My first word to all men and boys who care to hear me is "Don't get into debt. Starve and go to heaven — but don't borrow. Try first begging — I don't mind if it's really needful — stealing! But don't buy things you can't pay for!" And of all manner of debtors pious people building churches they can't pay for, are the most detestable nonsense to me. Can't you preach and pray behind the hedges — or in a sandpit — or a coalhole first? And of all manner of churches thus idiotically built, iron churches are the damnablest to me. And of all the sects and believers in any ruling spirit — Hindoos, Turks, Feather Idolaters, and Mumbo Jumbo, Log and Fire Worshippers — who want churches, your modern English Evangelical sect is the most absurd, and entirely objectionable and unendurable to me!

All which they might very easily have found out from my books — any other sort of sect would! — before bothering me to write it to them. Ever, nevertheless, and in all this saying, your faithful servant

JOHN RUSKIN

John Ruskin (1819-1900)

Ruskin's strictures against borrowing could well have been heeded by these two friends. Apparently the effort to recover a loan had gone past the subtle stage:

Sept 4 [1925]

I believe I am corrupting you: for when I first unmasked you — pulling the rock away and there you were, so to speak — you behaved in a very dignified and suitable way, didn't you?

... But I think you are deteriorating.... you are growing indecent.

You say, let the original arrangement stand: but where's the cheque, *old boy? Where's the esteemed favour that that arrangement arranged for? ... If you* can't *evacuate the six pounds, and if you are as constipated about a thing like that as you are about your food, well, tell me so, and there will be an end of the matter. Don't for the love of Mike get ill about it. But unless there is some natural obstruction of that sort, instead of saying let the arrangement stand,* do *something; sit down at your desk, draw out your cheque-book, write me a nice polite little note saying you are sorry there has been any trouble, close your eyes, hold your breath, and write* six — *and there you will be straight with me, at all events.*

Wyndham Lewis (1884-1957);
letter to O. R. Drey

Avoiding the borrower's touch has always called forth the utmost in ingenuity:

DEAR SON,
I am in prison for debt; come and assist your loving mother.
   E. FOOTE

DEAR MOTHER,
So am I; which prevents his duty being paid to his loving mother. —Your affectionate son,
   SAMUEL FOOTE
P.S. —*I have sent my attorney to assist you; in the meantime let us hope for better days.*

Samuel Foote (1720-1777)

MY DEAR SCROPE,
Lend me two hundred pounds. The banks are shut and all my

money is in the three per cents. It shall be repaid to-morrow morning. —*Yours,*

GEORGE BRUMMEL

MY DEAR GEORGE,
'Tis very unfortunate, but all my money is in the three per cents. —*Yours,*

S. DAVIES

George (Beau) Brummel (1778-1840)

'*BEAU*'*BRUMMEL*

and so has the writing of collection letters. The resolutely eccentric American painter James McNeill Whistler habitually gave his paintings such exotic titles as *Arrangement in Black and White* or *Harmony in Grey and Green*. The secretary of his London club, despairing of a long-overdue bill, finally hit the mark:

Dear Mr. Whistler:
It is not a Nocturne in Purple *or a* Symphony in Blue and Grey
we are after, but an Arrangement in Gold and Silver.

Whistler paid up, of course.

Violations of the code of proper and civilized conduct have had
a curious ability to arouse a most uncivilized ire. Oscar Wilde,
usually so urbane in conversation, fired off a genuinely outraged
letter when a journalist included some of his personal conversations in a book of anecdotes. The thing just wasn't gentlemanly!

> *I was not asking you to do me a favour; I was asserting my
> right to prevent my name being in any way associated with
> a book that . . . I consider extremely vulgar and offensive. No
> one has the right to make one godfather to a dirty baby against
> one's will. . . . I should be sorry to think that any Cambridge
> man could be wilfully guilty of such conduct, conduct which
> combines the inaccuracy of the eavesdropper with the method
> of the blackmailer.*
>
> Oscar Wilde (1854-1900); letter to Herbert Vivian

William Thackeray took similar umbrage when an acquaintance
retailed versions of his conversations in a series of "Literary Talk"
columns. The offense was compounded by having been committed in that most holy of sanctums — a gentleman's club:

> *We meet at a Club, where, before you were born I believe, I
> and other gentlemen have been in the habit of talking without
> any idea that our conversation would supply paragraphs for
> professional vendors of "Literary Talk"; and I don't remember
> that out of that Club I have ever exchanged six words with you.
> Allow me to inform you that the talk which you have heard*

there is not intended for newspaper remark; and to beg — as I have a right to do — that you will refrain from printing comments upon my private conversations; that you will forego discussions, however blundering, upon my private affairs; and that you will henceforth please to consider any question of my personal truth and sincerity as quite out of the province of your criticism.

W. M. THACKERAY.

William Makepeace Thackeray (1811-1863);
letter to Edmund Yates

The gentleman's club had a code of behavior all its own. One of the most celebrated libel cases of the 1920s also centered around a letter from a club. The rumpus began when a young writer resurrected an old slur on the morals of the long-dead William Ewart Gladstone:

Gladstone ... founded the great tradition ... in public to speak the language of the highest and strictest principle, and in private to pursue and possess every sort of woman.

Peter Wright on William Ewart Gladstone

The next Earl Gladstone and his brother, sons of the Grand Old Man, rose to the defense with commendable directness:

Mr. Peter Wright,
Your garbage about Mr. Gladstone in "Portraits and Criticisms" has come to our knowledge. You are a liar. Because you slander a dead man, you are a coward. Because you think the public will accept invention from such as you, you are a fool.

GLADSTONE.

I associate myself with this letter.

H. N. GLADSTONE.

Unrepentant, Wright reproached the brothers for their unparliamentary zeal:

> *My Lord, —*
> *I am in receipt of your Lordship's outburst dated July 22nd. . . .*
> *My views are unshaken even by the impact of your Lordship's controversial language, which, if I may say so without impoliteness, must rather have been acquired by practice in your Lordship's pantry than by the exercise of your Lordship's talents for debate in the House of Lords.*
>
> PETER E. WRIGHT.
> *The Bath Club, Dover Street, W.*

It was that postscript that did him in. To calumniate the dead was unsporting; to do it from the Bath Club — unthinkable! His Lordship appealed to the secretary:

> *Dear Wilson Taylor,*
> *Mr. Peter Wright appears to be a member of the Bath Club. In a book he made a foul charge against my father. He elaborated this in a letter to the* Nation. *. . . He wrote on Bath Club notepaper. . . . It seems to me that this is a matter for the Committee.*
> *Sincerely yours,*
>
> GLADSTONE

> *My Dear Wilson Taylor,*
> *. . . I wrote to you because I was so indignant that the fellow was sheltering in my old Club, which, for my brother, myself and my wife becomes uninhabitable so long as it is polluted by his presence. . . . By his baseless attacks on my father he has wantonly and deliberately insulted the fellow members of his Club.*
>
> GLADSTONE

Lord Gladstone (1854-1930)

Wm. E. GLADSTONE

The committee, on cue, promptly expelled the cad, who there-
upon sued for restitution and for libel. He was restored to the
again polluted club but lost his libel suit ignominiously. Gladstone at last was vindicated — and the Bath Club had played its
role.

All of which nonsense is much at odds with the dignified
reproaches made to the citizens of Birmingham by one of the
pioneers of modern science. At the height of popular feeling
against the French Revolution, the mob had sacked his house:

July 19, 1791

MY LATE TOWNSMEN AND NEIGHBOURS,
*You have destroyed the most truly valuable and useful appa-
ratus of philosophical instruments that perhaps any individual,*

in this or any other country, was ever possessed of. . . . You have destroyed the Library corresponding to that apparatus . . . But what I feel far more, you have destroyed manuscripts which have been the result of the laborious study of many years, and which I shall never be able to recompense; and this has been done to one who never did, or imagined, you any harm.

In this business we are the sheep and you the wolves. We will preserve our character and hope you will change yours. At all events we return you blessings for curses, and hope that you shall soon return to that industry and those sober manners for which the inhabitants of Birmingham were formerly distinguished.

Yours faithfully,

J. PRIESTLEY

> Joseph Priestley (1733-1804);
> letter to the inhabitants of
> Birmingham

Twentieth-century letter writers have shown much less of this "more in sorrow than in anger" approach. There is a distinct tone of "you're another" as America's most caustic columnist taxes a rival for his thin skin:

You are far, far better on the give than on the take. No man in American history has denounced more different people than you have, or in more violent terms, and yet no man that I can recall complains more bitterly when he happens to be hit. Why not stop your caterwauling for a while, and try to play the game according to the rules?

> H. L. Mencken (1880-1956); letter
> to Upton Sinclair

and as a famous drama critic hotly disputes the meaning of a word with a popular lyricist:

Listen, you contumacious rat, don't throw your dreary tomes at me. I'll give you an elegant dinner ... and sing to you between the courses if you can produce one writer or speaker, with an ear for the English language ... who uses "disinterested" in the sense you are now trying to bolster up ... a ghetto barbarism I had previously thought confined to the vocabularies of Ben Hecht and Jed Harris.

Alexander Woollcott (1887-1943);
letter to Ira Gershwin

Modern literary gentlemen have even been known to slash, unsuccessfully, at each other's jugular:

August 21, 1919
... Although I recognize you as a man of wit I realize it is not of the spontaneous order. There is nothing of the Whistler about you. ... You, like the mills of God, grind slow, and I might add, grind exceedingly small. ...

I am ... at a loss to explain how you should so far forget your pose as to express [your feelings] in such a laborious and boorish fashion, exposing to my astonished understanding the indication of a nature so calculating, petty, malicious and uncivilized, in short so strangely sub-human, as to realize almost the popular estimate of your character ...

Paul Nash (1889-1946); letter to Wyndham Lewis

August 25 [1919]
I am distressed to find ... that I should have driven such a dignified gentleman into the lamentable lapse of a series of tu quoques. *But I might have known that would happen! I sprinkle myself with a few ashes. ... I must leave you for the present to ruminate on ... how back-biting, shittiness and every*

mean practice is the specialty of your "sub-human" and bestial
enemies (whom Yaveh confound!).

Wyndham Lewis (1884-1957) letter to Paul Nash

A relatively feeble slanging-match, compared to those engaged
in long ago by such combatants as Daniel O'Connell and Benjamin Disraeli. Admirers at first, the two fell out when the young
writer abandoned his Radical beginnings and ran as a Tory politician. The old Irishman castigated Disraeli's race and his mo-
tives. The younger man challenged O'Connell's long-suffering
son to a duel, which was refused; Disraeli turned to more pointed
weapons:

London, May 6 [1835]

Mr. O'Connell:
Although you have long placed yourself out of the pale of
civilization, still I am one who will not be insulted, even by
a Yahoo, without chastising it. When I read ... your virulent
attacks upon myself, and that your son was at the same mo-
ment paying the penalty of similar virulence to another in-
dividual on whom you had dropped your filth ... I called
upon your son to reassume his vicarious office of yielding
satisfaction for his shrinking sire. But it seems that gentleman
declines the consequences of your libertine harangues. ... Lis-
ten, then, to me.

If it had been possible for you to act like a gentleman, you
would have hesitated before you made your foul and insolent
comments ... I admire your scurrilous allusions to my origin.
It is quite clear that the "hereditary bondman" has already
forgotten the clank of his fetter. ... With regard to your taunts
as to my want of success in my election contests, permit me
to remind you that I had nothing to appeal to but the good
sense of the people ... My pecuniary resources, too, were lim-
ited; I am not one of those public beggars that we see swarming
with their obtrusive boxes in the chapels of your creed, nor am

I in possession of a princely revenue wrung from a starving race of fanatical slaves....

We shall meet at Philippi; and ... I will seize the first opportunity of inflicting upon you a castigation which will make you at the same time remember and repent the insults that you have lavished upon

BENJAMIN DISRAELI

Benjamin Disraeli (1804-1881)

Disraeli's nemesis, Gladstone — that unintentional instigator of the Bath Club affair — did not have to wait for death to be insulted by post. Upset at changes the Grand Old Man was proposing to the Welsh church, an anonymous correspondent compressed onto one small postcard all the verbosity of her race, unleavened by the slightest touch of Christian charity:

Cannes, March 15, 1893

Far away from my native Land, my bitter indignation as a Welshwoman prompts me to reproach you, you bad, wicked, false, treacherous Old Man! ... You have no conscience, but I pray that God may even yet give you one that will sorely smart and trouble you before you die. You pretend to be religious, you old hypocrite! that you may more successfully pander to the evil passions of the lowest and most ignorant of the Welsh people.... You think you will shine in History, but it will be a notoriety similar to that of Nero. I see someone pays you the unintentional compliment of comparing you to Pontius Pilate, and I am sorry, for Pilate, though a political time-server, was, with all his faults, a very respectable man in comparison with you.... You are certainly cleverer. So also is your lord and master the Devil. And I cannot regard it as sinful to hate and despise you, any more than it is sinful to abhor Him. So with full measure of contempt and detestation, accept these compliments from

"A DAUGHTER OF OLD WALES"   Anonymous letter to William
                                 Ewart Gladstone

Enough! Far better the terse, civilized restraint, the ironic gibe at family pretensions, of a John Bright, taunted by a Tory politician named Smith:

> *He may not know that he is ignorant, but he cannot be ignorant that he lies. . . . I think the speaker was named Smith. He is a discredit to the numerous family of that name.*
>
> John Bright (1811-1899)

Bravado, in letter writing as elsewhere, has its own reward. This rogue's effrontery clearly amused Charles II, but there is a glint of steel in the monarch's reply:

> KING CHARLES, —
> *One of your subjects, the other night, robbed me of forty pounds, for which I robbed another of the same sum, who has inhumanly sent me to Newgate, and he swears I shall be hanged; therefore, for your own sake, save my life, or you will lose one of the best seamen in your navy.*
>
> JACK SKIFTON

> JACK SKIFTON —
> *For this time I'll save thee from the gallows; but if hereafter thou art guilty of the like, by —— I'll have thee hanged, though the best seaman in my navy. — Thine,*
>
> CHARLES REX
>
> Charles II (1630-1685)

The gentle Charles Lamb was one of the greatest of English letter writers. Like many otherwise innoffensive people, he was never happier than when making critical fun of others — in this case his sister:

DEAR MISS H., —

Mary has such an invincible reluctance to any epistolary exertion, that I am sparing her a mortification by taking the pen from her. The plain truth is, she writes such a pimping, mean, detestable hand, that she is ashamed at the formation of her letters. There is an essential poverty and abjectness in the frame of them. They look like begging letters. . . . Her figures, 1, 2, 3, 4, &c., . . . are not figures, but figurantes; and the combined posse go staggering up and down shameless, as drunkards in the day-time. It is no better when she rules her paper. . . . A sort of unnatural parallel lines, that are perpetually threatening to meet; which, you know, is quite contrary to Euclid. Her very blots are not bold like this, [HERE A BOLD BLOT] but poor smears, half left in and half scratched out, with another smear left in their place. . . . I don't think she can make a corkscrew if she tried.

Charles Lamb (1775-1834) to Miss Hutchinson

Of course, critical comment is hardly confined to the purely personal letter, as any business can attest. Some customers will complain about anything. In these times of relative religious tolerance it is hard to imagine the depth of feeling that inspired this querulous complaint:

January 8, 1908

DEAR SIRS, —

I am sorry to return the Drawers, which are a trifle too small round the waist. At the expense of being considered bigoted, to tell you the truth, I do not like the Brand, although the material is excellent in quality.

The man whose likeness appears, "WOLSEY," was one under whom poor Protestants writhed, *and although you may say this is a small matter and of no importance, it indicates the*

Firm at least allowing such to go forth in these critical times is at least careless, if not genuine Roman Catholics, and a Feather will indicate which way the wind blows.

Again the buttons would be far better of linen instead of pearl. Please to send me others.

Believe me, Yours faithfully.

Anonymous

The character reference, beloved of prospective employers, provides a heaven-sent opportunity for ambiguous phrases and damning with faint praise. Sometimes, however, the applicant does himself in, as does this eternally optimistic but all too honest father, eager to secure an "interest" for his young hopeful:

To the Honourable Board of Directors of the East India Co.

GENTLEMEN,

I have a parcel of fine boys, but not much cash to provide for them. I had intended my eldest son for the Church, but I find he is more likely to kick a church down than support it. I sent him to the University, but he could not submit himself to the college rules, and, on being reproved by his tutors, he took it up in the light of an affair of honour, and threatened to call them to account for it. All my plans for his welfare being thus disconcerted, I asked him if he had formed any for himself; he replied, he meant to go to India. I then inquired if he had any interest, at which question he looked somewhat foolish, and replied in the negative. Now, gentlemen, I know no more of you than you do of me. I therefore may appear to you not much wiser than my son. I can only say that he is of Welsh extraction for many generations, and, as my first-born, I flatter myself, has not degenerated. He is six feet high, of an athletic make, and bold and intrepid as a lion. If you like to see him I will equip him as a gentleman, and, I am, Gentlemen, etc.

Anonymous letter to the East India Company

One may imagine with what guarded enthusiasm John Company regarded the advent of this lion-like, church-bashing young Taffy.

A character reference was also the genesis of a remarkable early-Victorian correspondence which demonstrated, had it been doubted, that women are equally adept as men at pointed incivility. The initial letter was innocent enough:

> *Lady Seymour presents her compliments to Lady Shuckburgh, and would be obliged to her for the character of Mary Stedman, who states that she lived twelve months, and still is, in Lady Shuckburgh's establishment. Can Mary Stedman cook plain dishes well? make bread? and is she honest, good-tempered, sober, willing, and cleanly? Lady Seymour would also like to know the reason why she leaves Lady Shuckburgh's service? Direct, under cover to Lord Seymour, Maiden Bradley.*

Lady Jane Seymour was the granddaughter of Richard Brinsley Sheridan, and had all the great dramatist's sparkle. Some time earlier, at a bizarre pseudo-medieval tournament led by Louis Napoleon, she had been chosen "Queen of Beauty" — a triumph that apparently galled at least one rival. To Lady Seymour's domestic inquiries was returned a disdainful reply:

> *Lady Shuckburgh presents her compliments to Lady Seymour. Her ladyship's note, dated October 28, only reached her yesterday, November 3. Lady Shuckburgh was unacquainted with the name of the kitchen-maid until mentioned by Lady Seymour, as it is her custom neither to apply for or give characters to any of the under servants, this being always done by the housekeeper, Mrs. Couch — and this was well known to the young woman; therefore Lady Shuckburgh is surprised at her referring any lady to her for a character. Lady Shuckburgh having a professed cook, as well as a housekeeper, in her*

> *establishment, it is not very likely she herself should know any-*
> *thing of the abilities or merits of the under servants; therefore*
> *she is unable to answer Lady Seymour's note. Lady Shuckburgh*
> *cannot imagine Mary Stedman to be capable of cooking for*
> *any except the servants'-hall table.*

Lady Seymour was too much her grandfather's granddaughter to
swallow such hoity-toity high-handedness. A casual misspelling
reveals the true Sheridan touch:

> *Lady Seymour presents her compliments to Lady Shuckburgh,*
> *and begs she will order her housekeeper, Mrs. Pouch, to send*
> *the girl's character without delay; otherwise another young*
> *woman will be sought for elsewhere, as Lady Seymour's chil-*
> *dren cannot remain without their dinners because Lady Shuck-*
> *burgh, keeping a "professed cook and a housekeeper", thinks*
> *a knowledge of the details of her establishment beneath her*
> *notice. Lady Seymour understands from Stedman that, in ad-*
> *dition to her other talents, she was actually capable of dressing*
> *food fit for the little Shuckburghs to partake of when hungry.*

Appended to this missive was a pen and ink cartoon of the three
Shuckburgh children, with large heads and cauliflower wigs, slav-
ering over a chop prepared by a grinning Mary Stedman, while
their mother hovered in dismay.

This was too much for offended dignity. The attempted
squelch-by-proxy, when it came, managed to reveal the true cause
of Lady Shuckburgh's pique:

> MADAM,
> *Lady Shuckburgh has directed me to acquaint you that she*
> *declines answering your note, the vulgarity of which is beneath*
> *contempt; and although it may be the characteristic of the*
> *Sheridans to be vulgar, coarse, and witty, it is not that of a*

"lady", unless she happens to have been born in a garret and bred in a kitchen. Mary Stedman informs me that your ladyship does not keep either a cook or a housekeeper, and that you only require a girl who can cook a mutton chop. If so, I apprehend that Mary Stedman, or any other scullion, will be found fully equal to cook for or manage the establishment of the Queen of Beauty. I am, your Ladyship, &c.,

ELIZABETH COUCH *(not Pouch).*

The correspondence was at an end. One supposes that Stedman was soon cooking mutton chops for small descendants of Sheridan, and that the honors, if any, went to the Queen of Beauty.

MY DEAR SIR,
I have read your play.
Oh, my dear Sir.
Yours Faithfully
HERBERT BEERBOHM TREE

Sir Herbert Beerbohm Tree (1853-1917) to a would-be dramatist

CHAPTER THREE

Three Curmudgeons and a Canon

CURMUDGEON: *A testy, grumpy, gruff, irascible man; a grouch.*

W.S. LANDOR

Wm. COBBETT

DUKE of WELLINGTON

We all know them. People whose instinct is to criticize; who are quick to give and take offense; whose habitual frame of mind is irritation — people who can lay claim to the name curmudgeon. But only occasionally does someone arise whose breathtaking bloody-mindedness and captivating cantankerousness combine with an inspired ability to put them into words. For lovers of malicious wit, true curmudgeons have such an irresistible charm that they deserve to be immortalized in some left-handed Hall of Fame.

Three contumacious curmudgeons, now largely forgotten, have a particular appeal today. Although they were contemporaries, they were very different men. William Cobbett was a politician, pamphleteer and journalist who crusaded against social and political injustice in language so extreme that today it is difficult to credit. The duke of Wellington was the victorious general of the Battle of Waterloo. As curt and blunt as Cobbett was long-winded, Wellington was a staunch defender of the status quo who did not know the meaning of the word tact and who never suffered a fool in his life. Walter Savage Landor was a much less public figure, a fierce old literary gentleman with a formidable temper, who never missed a chance to take arms against a sea of real or imagined foes.

Like us, these curmudgeons lived through a time of momentous and bewildering change. They experienced the American and French revolutions, the twenty long years of the Napoleonic wars, and the transformation of England from a rural to an industrial nation. And although their reactions to these events were totally different, they shared the supreme egotism of knowing that they were always right, and their fellow men always wrong.

The Watchdog
William Cobbett (1763-1835)

The very quintessence of a curmudgeon was William Cobbett. Cobbett was an extraordinary man — a soldier, a crusading journalist, a rabble-rousing Radical politician, a teacher, an agricultural experimenter, and always a man of violent and eccentric opinions. As prickly as his pseudonym, "Peter Porcupine," implied, he was one of those people who are naturally "anti."

Cobbett looked like John Bull and acted like Don Quixote, riding the length and breadth of England tilting at the windmills of injustice. In words as vigorous and powerful as they were intemperate, he flailed away at men in power and out of power, at new opinions and old ideas, never reckoning the consequences and never minding where his incendiary packages landed. Civilized and dignified men found him a bit heavy-handed:

> *A Philistine with six fingers on every hand and on every foot six toes, four and twenty in number: a Philistine the shaft of whose spear is like a weaver's beam.*
>
> Matthew Arnold (1822-1888) on
> William Cobbett

Cobbett was like a bomb bursting in air — spectacular but with few lasting results. He had exploded on the scene as a young pamphleteer horrified by the ideas behind the American and French revolutions:

> *How Thomas Paine gets a living now, or what brothel he inhabits I know not. . . . Like Judas he will be remembered by*

*posterity; men will learn to express all that is base, malignant,
treacherous, unnatural and blasphemous by the single mono-
syllable — Paine.*

On Thomas Paine

In one of the many 180-degree turns that marked his career,
Cobbett later became a passionate advocate of many of those
same ideas. To atone for his attacks on Paine, he removed the
English-born revolutionary's mortal remains from the unhal-
lowed ground where they were buried in America, with some
hazy notion of erecting a memorial in England. The plan fizzled;
the bones lay forgotten for many years in a suitcase in Cobbett's
house, and on his death they disappeared forever. The whole
bizarre episode provided a field day for the doggerel writers:

> *Cobbett, through all his life a cheat,*
> *Yet as a rogue was incomplete,*
> *For now to prove a finished knave*
> *To dupe and trick, he robs a grave.*

Anonymous, 1818

> *In digging up your bones, Tom Paine,*
> *Will. Cobbett has done well:*
> *You visit him on earth again,*
> *He'll visit you in Hell.*

Lord Byron (1788-1824)

Cobbett was at bottom a romantic conservative fighting desper-
ately to restore the overidealized rural England he loved. He
abhorred the corrupt political "System" which, of course, was
responsible for every social evil. And he despised the new financial powers and the rise of the stock exchange, which he
christened with typical venom:

The Muckworm is no longer a creeping thing: it rears its head aloft, and makes the haughty Borough Lords sneak about in holes and corners.

Cobbett also vented his wrath on the new type of country squires, who cared nothing for their workers or the poor:

> *These incomparable cowards; these wretched slaves; these dirty creatures who call themselves country gentlemen, deserve ten times as much as they have yet had to suffer....*
> *The foul, the stinking, the carrion baseness, of the fellows ...*

He deplored the growing gulf between rich and poor in England, and contrasted the plight of the laborer with the life-style of the social-climbing rich farmer:

> *A fox-hunting horse; polished boots; a spanking trot to market; a "Get out of the way or by G-d I'll ride over you" to every poor devil upon the road; wine at his dinner; a servant (and sometimes in* livery) *to wait at his table; a painted lady for a wife; sons aping the young 'squires and lords; a house crammed up with sofas, pianos, and all sorts of fooleries.*

To Cobbett, cities were a blot on the earth — London he always referred to as "the Great Wen." One day he passed through Cheltenham, a fashionable spa:

> *Which is what they call a "watering-place"; that is to say, a place to which East India plunderers, West India floggers, English tax-gorgers, together with gluttons, drunkards, and debauchees of all descriptions, female as well as male, resort, at the suggestion of silently laughing quacks, in the hope of getting rid of the bodily consequences of their manifold sins and iniquities.... To places like this come all that is knavish and all that is foolish and all that is base; gamesters, pick-pockets, and*

harlots; young wife-hunters in search of rich and ugly old women, and young husband-hunters in search of rich and wrinkled or half-rotten men, the former resolutely bent, be the means what they may, to give the latter heirs to their lands and tenements.

On Cheltenham

Cobbett's greatest charm was his diversity. Never single-minded, he tended to ride off in all directions at once. A discussion of political reform would suddenly become a diatribe against classical authors:

Those base, servile, self-degraded wretches, Virgil and Horace.

A crawling and disgusting parasite, a base scoundrel, and pandar to unnatural passion.

On Virgil

or an attack on the nation's literary giants:

Indeed, the whole of Milton's poem is such barbarous trash, so outrageously offensive to reason and to common sense that one is naturally led to wonder how it can have been tolerated by a people, amongst whom astronomy, navigation, and chemistry are understood.

On *Paradise Lost*

or a vilification of the fashionable musicians who infested the cities:

Squeaking wretches who have consumed this year two or three thousand quarters of corn.

The singers and their crew are not only useless in themselves, but spread about at large their contagious effeminacy.

On Italian singers in London

Many of his notions were nothing if not eccentric. He damned tea as a pallid and evil beverage that would weaken England's moral fiber:

The gossip of the tea table is no bad preparatory school for the brothel.

and never missed an opportunity to denounce that most despicable of all plants, the humble potato. In the good old days, such rubbish had not polluted the table of the farm worker; but now

his beer and his bread and meat are . . . exchanged for the cat-lap of the tea-kettle, taxed to more than three-fourths of its prime cost, and for the cold and heartless diet of the potato plant.

Ranging far and wide, Cobbett could work up the most astonishing head of steam against historical figures who had been dead for over 200 years:

A name which deserves to be held in everlasting execration; a name which we could not pronounce without almost doubting of the justice of God, were it not for our knowledge of the fact, that the cold-blooded, most perfidious, most impious, most blasphemous caitiff expired at last, amidst those flames which he himself had been the chief cause of kindling.
On Archbishop Thomas Cranmer

and against literary sacred cows. Cobbett had supreme confidence in his ability to set all things right:

Dr. Dread-Devil . . . said that there were no trees in Scotland. I wonder how they managed to take him around without letting him see trees. I suppose that lick-spittle Boswell, or Mrs. Piozzi, tied a bandage over his eyes when he went over the country which I have been over. I shall sweep away all this bundle of lies.

On Samuel Johnson

His contemporaries fared no better. Pitt, for instance, the chief exponent of "the System":

The great snorting bawler.

On William Pitt

or a passing chief minister:

What will now be said to this cowardly crowing of pompous chanticleer upon his own dunghill?

On Henry Addington, Viscount Sidmouth

or an execrable monarch:

As a son, as a husband, as a father, and especially as an advisor of young men, I deem it my duty to say that, on a review of his whole life, I can find no one good thing to speak of, in either the conduct or character of this king.

On George IV

When it came to women, there was a curious streak of Mrs. Grundy in Cobbett. S-E-X was a word not to be mentioned. What is one to make, for instance, of his opposition to wet-nurses, who allow a new mother:

... to hasten back, *unbridled and undisfigured, to those enjoyments, to have an eagerness for which, a really delicate woman will shudder at the thought of being suspected.*

or even to the remarriage of a widow, who has:

> ... a second time *undergone that surrender, to which nothing but the most ardent affection could ever reconcile a chaste and delicate woman.*

Cobbett could never distinguish between people and their ideas, and he translated his disapproval of Malthus's theories into a violent hatred of the man:

> *Parson,*
> *I have during my life, detested many men; but never any one so much as you. ... Priests have, in all ages, been remarkable for cool and deliberate and unrelenting cruelty; but it seems to be reserved for the Church of England to produce one who has a just claim to the atrocious pre-eminence. No assemblage of words can give an appropriate designation of you; and therefore, as being the single word which best suits the character of such a man, I call you Parson, which, amongst other meanings, includes that of Boroughmonger's Tool.*
>
> To Thomas Malthus

Although he did become an MP, Cobbett achieved less than many had expected. It took an observant foreigner to explain why:

> *He is a chained house-dog who falls with equal fury on every one whom he does not know, often bites the best friend of the house, barks incessantly, and just because of this incessantness of his barking cannot get listened to, even when he barks at an actual thief. Therefore the distinguished thieves who plunder England do not think it necessary to throw the growling Cobbett a bone to stop his mouth. This makes the dog furiously savage, and he shows all his hungry teeth. Poor old Cobbett! England's watch-dog!*
>
> Heinrich Heine (1797-1856) on William Cobbett

The Iron Duke
The duke of Wellington
(1769-1852)

A minor but memorable figure in the ranks of curmudgeonry was Arthur Wellesley, duke of Wellington. Victor of Waterloo, prime minister of Great Britain, field marshal of the army, the Iron Duke was in his way a legendary and epic character. Crusty, testy and irascible he certainly was, but unlike most of his fellow curmudgeons he was a man of remarkably few words, and his gruff terseness became his trademark. Speaking of another prime minister, he once barked:

I have no small talk and Peel has no manners.
On Robert Peel

Permitting no liberties and given to calling a spade a spade, the duke was nothing if not blunt. When a lady with more familiarity than good sense inquired whether he had been surprised to discover he had won the Battle of Waterloo, he replied frigidly:

By God! not half as much surprised as I am right now, mum.

At the height of his considerable fame, which he accepted as only his due, a stranger approached him in the street:

STRANGER: *Mr. Robinson, I believe?*
WELLINGTON: *Sir, if you believe that you'll believe anything.*

Having in one instance against his will accepted the arm of a passerby in crossing the street, he listened with impatience as the stranger burbled his pleasure in helping the victor of Waterloo, then grunted:

Don't be a damned fool

and turned on his heel. The old warrior had no illusions about the value of military glory:

There is nothing worse than a defeat except a victory.

and even fewer about the kind of spectacular heroism appreciated by the crowd:

There is nothing on earth so stupid as a gallant officer.

Perverse as always, Wellington heaped scorn on the elite troops of the army, the cavalry.

The only thing that they can be relied on to do is to gallop too far and too fast.

When a detachment of fresh young officers arrived at his camp during the Peninsular War, he eyed them with something less than enthusiasm:

I don't know what effect they will have upon the enemy, but by God, they frighten me!

Much as he disapproved of all his troops, Wellington despised the victorious army of Waterloo most:

The scum of the earth — they have enlisted for drink, that is the simple truth.

The most infamous army I ever commanded.

Utter unflappability was one of the duke's most visible qualities. On the field of Waterloo he rode with his second-in-command as the musket balls whistled by:

LORD UXBRIDGE: *By God, there goes my leg!*
WELLINGTON: *By God, so it does.*

and while he respected his chief opponent, he found one of his qualities regrettable:

He is no gentleman.

> On Napoleon Bonaparte

The French, in turn, didn't think much of Wellington:

Waterloo was a battle of the first rank won by a captain of the second.

> Victor Hugo on the duke of Wellington

Congenitally opposed to anything newfangled, he had no patience with modern trends in music. As ambassador in Vienna he suffered through a performance of Beethoven's *The Battle of Vitoria,* and when asked by a Russian diplomat whether the music resembled the real battle:

By God, no, if it had been, I should have run away myself.

> On Beethoven's *The Battle of Vitoria*

Wellington's gradual involvement in politics threw him into contact with the reigning House of Hanover. Apparently oblivious of his own habitual profanity, he disapproved strongly of the dissolute prince regent:

By God, you never saw such a figure in your life as he is. Then he speaks and swears so like old Falstaff, that damn me if I am not ashamed to walk into a room with him.

> On the prince regent (later
> George IV)

The prince's wife, later Queen Caroline, was also a favorite with the duke:

CAROLINE: *You see how punctual I am, Duke; I am even before my time.*

WELLINGTON: *That, your majesty, is not punctuality.*

Caroline, accused by her profligate husband of many and flagrant infidelities, became the centre of a violent public controversy. At its height she was urged by a pompous preacher to "Go, and sin no more." Popular doggerel took up the cry:

Most Gracious Queen, we thee implore
To go away and sin no more,
But if that effort be too great,
To go away at any rate.

> Anonymous; on Queen Caroline

The London mob supported the queen, so Wellington, typically, opted for the king. Driving through the City, he was set upon by a gaggle of workmen who refused to let him pass until he pronounced "God Save the Queen." The duke shrugged:

Well, gentlemen, since you will have it so — "God save the Queen"; and may all your wives be like her!

> The duke of Wellington (1769-1852) on Queen Caroline

The Iron Duke went on to become one of the most reactionary prime ministers in history, inveighing against the popular agitation for political change. He was appalled by the members of the newly reformed House of Commons:

I never saw so many shocking bad hats in my life.

Nevertheless, he was a shrewd and sometimes cynical politician. Of a singularly uninspired minister he noted:

Oh! He is a very good bridge for rats to run over.
On William Huskisson

The duke spent so much time away from home that he became a stranger to his family. His children were something of a trial to him, particularly the eldest, Lord Douro, who was extraordinarily like him:

There is only one caricature of me that has ever caused me annoyance: Douro.

The Iron Duke never had the least doubt of his own self-worth or place in the world. The French marshals, chagrined at their defeat by an inferior, turned their backs on him at Vienna. To a sympathetic onlooker, the duke smiled his frosty smile:

Madam, I have seen their backs before.
The duke of Wellington (1769-1852)

The Old Lion
Walter Savage Landor
(1775-1864)

A curmudgeon of a character very different from either Cobbett or Wellington was the aptly named Walter Savage Landor. Landor is remembered now chiefly as a minor poet and essayist, a classicist who wrote much of his poetry in Latin and translated it into English and an accomplished stylist whose balanced, periodic sentences are reminiscent of Dr. Johnson's. But in his own day he was the Old Lion, celebrated for his growl. Aristocratic, snobbish, serenely self-confident and self-important, Landor was one of those people who see personal affront everywhere. A lifelong series of wrangles with one adversary after another culminated in his virtual exile from England in late middle age as the result of a libel suit. He was possessed of an extravagant and ungovernable temper which tended to explode in all directions. The unpredictable fallout might descend anywhere — on the luckless architect of his Welsh farmhouse:

> *The earth contains no race of human beings so totally vile and worthless as the Welsh ... I have expended in labour, within three years, eight thousand pounds amongst them, and yet they treat me as their greatest enemy ...*
>
> Letter to Robert Southey

— or on the head of his not undeserving publisher, John Taylor, who had scissored some typically controversial passages from a Landor manuscript:

> *His first villany ... instigated me to throw my fourth volume, in its imperfect state, into the fire, and has cost me nine-tenths*

of my fame as a writer. His next villany will entail perhaps a chancery-suit on my children, — for at its commencement I blow my brains out . . . This cures me forever, if I live, of writing what could be published . . . Not a line of any kind shall I leave behind me. My children shall be carefully warned against literature. To fence, to swim, to speak French, are the most they shall learn.

Letter to Robert Southey

Landor had a high opinion of himself as a writer and of the supreme importance of writers in general. But he took a jaundiced view of authors themselves, both contemporary and remote — Byron, for instance:

Byron dealt chiefly in felt and furbelow, wavy Damascus daggers, and pocket pistols studded with paste. He threw out frequent and brilliant sparks; but his fire burnt to no purpose; it blazed furiously when it caught muslin, and it hurried many a pretty wearer into an untimely blanket.

On Lord Byron

— and Shakespeare:

Not a single one [of the sonnets] is very admirable. . . . They are hot and pothery: there is much condensation, little delicacy; like raspberry jam without cream, without crust, without bread.

On Shakespeare's sonnets

Never one to overvalue consistency, Landor also castigated those who didn't appreciate Shakespeare enough! An eye witness described the Old Lion in full flight:

During one of the sittings the artist happened to speak enthusiastically about some lines of Ben Jonson, whereupon Mr. Landor, who was seated at the time, bounded from his chair, and began pacing the room and shaking his tightly clenched

*hands as he thundered out "Ben Jonson! Not another word
about him! It makes my blood boil! I haven't patience to hear
the fellow's name. A pigmy! an upstart! a presumptuous varlet
who dared to be thought more of than Shakespeare was in his
day!" "But surely," ventured the artist, "that was not poor Ben
Jonson's fault, but the fault of the undiscriminating generation
in which they both lived." "Not at all!" roared Landor, his
eyeballs becoming bloodshot and his nostrils dilating, "not at
all! The fellow should have walled himself up in his own brick
and mortar before he had connived at and allowed such sacrilege!" "But!," said I — for the painter could not speak for
laughter — "even if Ben Jonson had been able to achieve such
a tour de force, I am very certain, Mr. Landor, that Shakespeare
would have been the very first to pull down his friend's hand-
iwork and restore him to the world." "No such thing!" rejoined
Mr. Landor, turning fiercely upon me; "Shakespeare never
wasted his time; and with his woonderful imagination, he'd
have known he could have created fifty better."*

Lady Bulwer-Lytton (1802-1882)
on Walter Savage Landor

One of Landor's favorite targets was Wordsworth. An early ad-
mirer of the Lake poet, Landor soon took umbrage at Wordsworth's egotism and his alleged mistreatment of his fellow poet
Robert Southey. Henceforth he seldom missed an opportunity
to aim a well-turned metaphor:

> *The surface of Wordsworth's mind, the poetry, has a good deal
> of staple about it, and will bear handling; but the inner, the
> conversational and private, has many coarse intractable dan-
> gling threads, fit only for the flockbed equipage of grooms.*

On William Wordsworth

Ultrasensitive to criticism himself, Landor inveighed against the
literary critics, particularly those of the *Edinburgh Review*. Even

the Old Lion was unable to bring much ill nature to bear on th
rotund and amiable Sydney Smith:

Humour's pink Primate, Sydney Smith

He reserved the full vigor of his plain speaking for the mos
visible of the *Review*ers, Henry Brougham, who had long sinc
risen to the eminence of lord chancellor. Vain and ambitious
Brougham had been incautious enough to sue a London pape
for libel. Landor fired off a withering denunciation to the editor

> SIR: *The prosecution with which you are threatened by Lord
> Brougham might well be expected from every facette of hi
> polygonal character. . . . In the days when Brougham and hi
> confederates were writers in [the Edinburgh Review], more
> falsehood and malignity marked its pages than any other Jour
> nal in the language. . . .*
>
> *What other man within the walls of Parliament, however
> hasty, rude, and petulant, hath exhibited such manifold in
> stances of bad manners, bad feelings, bad reasonings, bad
> language, and bad law?*

On Henry, Lord Brougham

Republican in sentiment since the days of his youth, Landor regarded the momentous political events of his time with a cynical
and fastidious eye. But when William IV's ministers removed from
Coleridge the miserly state pension awarded by George IV, Landor was able to rouse himself to something like his customary
level of indignation:

> *George IV, the vilest wretch in Europe, gave him £100 a year,
> enough, in London, to buy three turnips and half an egg a
> day. Those men were surely the most dexterous of courtiers,*

who resolved to shew William that his brother was not the vilest, by dashing the half egg and three turnips from the plate of Coleridge. No such action as this is recorded of any administration in the British annals, and I am convinced that there is not a state in Europe, or Asia, in which the paltriest minister of the puniest despot would recommend it.

Landor had once used his gift for deadly doggerel to pin the wings of the Hanoverian Georges; years later he did the same for the British military with his immortal couplet on the Crimean War:

Hail, you indomitable heroes, hail!
Despite of all your generals, ye prevail.

In spite of his irascibility, or because of it, Landor managed to retain a number of fast friends who bomb-proofed themselves against occasional mortar fire and were sometimes even able to return it. Once, when Landor was violently attacking, of all things, the Psalms, Lady Blessington smiled sweetly and cooed:

Do write something better, Mr. Landor.
> Marguerite, Countess Blessington
> (1789-1849)

Definitely a low blow. After receiving a missive with a pointed invitation, Charles Dickens took a fiendish delight in turning the other cheek:

YOUNG MAN, — *I will not go there if I can help it. I have not the least confidence in the value of your introduction to the Devil. . . . If you were the man I took you for . . . you would come to Paris and amaze the weak walls of the house I haven't found yet with that steady snore of yours, which I once heard piercing the door of your bedroom in Devonshire Terrace,*

reverberating along the bell wire in the hall, so getting outside into the street, playing Aeolian harps among the area railings, and going down the New Road like the blast of a trumpet.

I forgive you your reviling of me: there's a shovelful of live coals for your head — does it burn? And am, with true affection — does it burn now? — Ever yours.

Charles Dickens (1812-1870);
letter to Walter Savage Landor

The rampant Old Lion, capable of instant and extravagant rage, is seen in full roar in what can only be interpreted as a challenge to a duel with a lawyer who had been a conspicuously bad samaritan. The contrast between the triviality of the offense and the formality of the classical style is almost ludicrous. The balanced sentences, the Latin tag, the snobbery, the casual aspersions on his victim's breeding, learning and professional capacity — all are Landor at his most typical:

Permit me, Sir, to recall to your memory your insulting language and violent demeanor of yesterday . . . I had just taken refuge from the rain under your verandah, when I heard the following words, uttered with a coarseness and vehemence I had never heard before from any well-dressed man on any occasion. "What do you want here? Be off with you." Until I heard the latter phrase spoken close to me, I did not imagine or suspect that it was addressed to me. On my asking you . . . whether it was so, you answered in the affirmative, and still more offensively. I . . . reminded you that such language was not usually applied to a gentleman. You expressed a doubt whether I am one. I gave you all the benefit of that doubt, knowing that only a gentleman can judge of one correctly.

But I thought my manner, my language, and my tone, were unexceptionable, and (what you are more capable of appreciating) my dress. It is that in which, during last week, I had visited several of the first families in Cornwall . . . in whose society you will never be admitted, unless (to their sorrow) professionally. . . . In your terms and utterance there was what Cicero calls subrancidum nescio quid. *The curate of your parish will explain this to you. . . . I caused no obstruction: I stood several feet from the doorway, and with my back toward it. On my expostulating, you not only repeated the same insolence of expression, but you advanced in a menacing and outrageous attitude.*

There is no great bravery in thus insulting a man of seventy-three, without a cane or whip in his hand: but the man of seventy-three has not yet forgotten, in case of necessity and in a proper time and place, to repel a ruffian and to spurn a coward.

Letter to James Jerwood

Landor could, when he chose, be brief. All his sense of dignity and self-worth is summoned up in this icy rebuke to a political lordling who had cut him dead at Florence; its closing is the essential Walter Savage Landor:

MY LORD, — *Now I am recovering from an illness of several months' duration, aggravated no little by your lordship's rude reception of me at the Cascine, in presence of my family and innumerable Florentines. I must remind you in the gentlest terms of the occurrence.*

We are both of us old men, my lord, and are verging on decrepitude and imbecility. Else my note might be more energetic. I am not unobservant of distinctions. You, by the favour of a Minister, are Marquis of Normanby; I by the grace of God am

WALTER SAVAGE LANDOR.

Walter Savage Landor (1775-
1864); letter to the marquis of
Normanby

The Canon of Wit
Sydney Smith (1771-1845)

SYDNEY SMITH

Periodically there comes along one of those rare souls who transcend their own time — whose brilliance and wit charm every generation, and who continue to speak in words that seem fresh and modern. The Reverend Sydney Smith was such a man. He was the very opposite of a curmudgeon — a high-spirited and convivial man who never failed to see the essential comedy of the human condition. Captivating he most certainly was, but not in the conventional sense. A huge, Falstaffian figure,

*What a hideous, odd-looking man Sydney Smith is! with a
mouth like an oyster, and three double-chins.*

Mrs. Brookfield on Sydney Smith

he allowed his expansive wit full play as, without malice but with
finely pointed humor and ridicule, he punctured the reputations
of the pompous and assailed the works of the vain and stupid.

In his day, Sydney Smith was acknowledged as the wittiest man
in England. For over forty years he dominated London society
with his exhilarating conversation and the force of his jovial
personality, in spite of the fact that in all that time he was rarely
in the city more than one or two months a year. But there was
much more than this to Sydney Smith. As canon of St. Paul's
Cathedral he reorganized the cathedral's doddering finances. He
was an exemplary country parson and a brilliant preacher. He
was perhaps one of the two or three greatest letter writers the
English language has ever produced. He was cofounder of the
Edinburgh Review, a journal whose influence on four generations
of Englishmen was incalculable. And as a political reformer and
adviser to prime ministers and statesmen, his effect on nineteenth-century English political and social life was greater than
has ever been acknowledged.

The essence of Sydney Smith's wit lay in his imagination. Both
he and his listeners would shake with laughter as, seized with
an idea, he piled one flight of ludicrous fancy on another. He
was informed one day that a young Scot of his acquaintance was
engaged to marry a widow twice his age, whose dimensions
rivaled Sydney's own:

*Going to marry her! Going to marry her! impossible! you mean,
a part of her; he could not marry her all himself. It would be
a case, not of bigamy, but of trigamy; the neighbourhood or
the magistrates should interfere. There is enough of her to
furnish wives for a whole parish. One man marry her! — it is*

monstrous. You might people a colony with her; or give an assembly with her; or perhaps take your morning walks around her, always providing there were frequent resting places, and you are in rude health. I once was rash enough to try walking round her before breakfast, but only got half-way and gave it up exhausted. Or you might read the Riot Act and disperse her; in short, you might do anything with her but marry her.

Less spontaneous but equally typical and ridiculous was Smith's speculation on the metaphysical significance of tropical birds. As with so many of his apparently light-hearted comparisons, the sting is in the tail:

The toucan has an enormous bill, makes a noise like a puppy dog, and lays his eggs in hollow trees. How astonishing are the freaks and fancies of nature! To what purpose, we say, is a bird placed in the woods of Cayenne with a bill a yard long, making noise like a puppy dog, and laying eggs in hollow trees? The toucans, to be sure, might retort, to what purpose were gentlemen in Bond Street created? To what purpose were certain foolish Members of Parliament created? — pestering the House of Commons with their ignorance and folly, and impeding the business of the country? There is no end of such questions. So we will not enter into the metaphysics of the toucan.

Although Smith was celebrated for his wit and humor, it was his tragedy that his enormous talents were never fully utilized because the solemn and serious men in power could not bring themselves to trust him. He was too independent — too irreverent — and just too damned funny!

Sydney Smith's ambition was to be a lawyer, but poverty and his father's insistence drove him into the Church. During a brief stint as a tutor in Edinburgh he helped found the *Edinburgh*

Review; afterwards he made something of a splash in London society. But then his finances forced him to accept a twenty-year exile to a poor country-living in the north of England. To a man of Smith's urbanity and gregarious nature, life in the country was akin to the grave:

> *Whenever I enter a village, straightway I find an ass.*

Unlike Cobbett, he had no romantic notions about the virtues of rural society. He dealt too much with the poor to idealize them:

> *A ploughman marries a ploughwoman because she is plump; generally uses her ill; thinks his children an encumbrance; very often flogs them; and, for sentiment, has nothing more nearly approaching to it than the ideas of broiled bacon and mashed potatoes.*

He contemplated with irony the fate of Jean Jacques Rousseau, the prophet of the natural life, condemned to a rural estate by his patroness, Madame d'Epinay:

> *Among the real inhabitants of the country, the reputation of reading and thinking is fatal to character; and Jean Jacques cursed his own successful eloquence which had sent him from the suppers and flattery of Paris to smell daffodils, watch sparrows, or project idle saliva into the passing stream.*

One might have expected such a man to become despondent. But Smith, to the amazement and amusement of his friends, plunged into the agricultural life with vigor, while still finding time to read, keep up a wide correspondence, write vigorously for the *Review,* and captivate London on his brief annual forays.

Smith's tenure in Edinburgh had left him with an exasperated admiration for the Scots. Thereafter he could never resist the opportunity to poke fun at them, and many a letter or article was enlivened by an offhand dig:

> *It requires a surgical operation to get a joke well into a Scotch understanding. Their only idea of wit, or rather that inferior variety of this electric talent which prevails occasionally in the north, and which, under the name of wut, is so infinitely distressing to people of good taste, is laughing immoderately at stated intervals.*

> *[Palmerston's] manner when speaking is like a man washing his hands; the Scotch members don't know what he is doing.*

> *That garret of the earth — the knuckle-end of England — that land of Calvin, oat-cakes and sulphur.*

Not that Sydney had any illusions about the national character of his own people:

> *It must be acknowledged that the English are the most disagreeable of all the nations of Europe — more surly and morose, with less disposition to please, to exert themselves for the good of society, to make small sacrifices, and to put themselves out of their way.*

In Paris he was embarrassed by the spectacle of the Ugly Englishman:

> *The house was full of English, who talk loud and seem to care little for other people. This is their characteristic, and a very brutal and barbarous distinction it is.*

Smith knew the Americans only at second remove. Like many an Englishman, he was inclined to undervalue them:

In the four corners of the globe, who reads an American book?
or goes to an American play? or looks at an American picture
or statue? What does the world yet owe to American physicians
or surgeons? .. Who drinks out of American glasses? or eats
from American plates? or wears American coats or gowns? or
sleeps in American blankets? Finally, under which of the old
tyrannical governments of Europe is every sixth man a slave,
whom his fellow creatures may buy and sell and torture?

He was distressed by a habit which had been remarked by countless English travelers:

We are terribly afraid that some Americans spit on the floor,
even when that floor is covered by good carpets. Now all claims
to civilization are suspended till this secretion is otherwise
disposed of. No English gentleman has spit upon the floor since
the Heptarchy.

Smith had several later altercations with the Americans, and they
ultimately retaliated by consistently spelling his name *Sidney*!
  Smith was intensely ambitious, but he recognized that his own
habits of mind did not mark him for preferment in his profession:

In the Church, if you are not well born, you must be very base
or very foolish, or both.

Sydney was neither. In common with many others, he did not
hold a high opinion of the average clergyman:

SQUIRE: *If I had a son who was an idiot, by Jove, I'd make him*
a parson!
SMITH: *Very probably; but I see that your father was of a different*
mind.

The Church of England in the nineteenth century was almost a branch of the civil service, and high clerical appointments were inevitably political. In spite of his significant services to social and political reform, his Whig friends, when they came to power, did not choose to make him a bishop. Sydney was too likely to say what he thought. He was a man of conscience who could not be relied upon to toe the line. He was finally elevated to the position of canon of St. Paul's, but watched lesser men appointed to the bench of bishops.

Smith was deeply disappointed, but the man was incapable of bitterness. He would have been less than human, however, had he not seized every opportunity to tweak the ear of the bishops; sometimes with high seriousness:

> It is a melancholy thing to see a man, clothed in soft raiment, lodged in a public palace, endowed with a rich portion of the product of other men's industry, using all the influence of his splendid situation, however conscientiously, to deepen the ignorance, and inflame the fury, of his fellow creatures.

but more often in the tongue-in-cheek style that was his trademark:

> I must believe in the Apostolic Succession, there being no other way of accounting for the descent of the Bishop of Exeter from Judas Iscariot.

> How can a bishop marry? How can he flirt? The most he can say is, "I will meet you in the vestry after service."

Sydney Smith was intensely involved in the social and political movements of his day — always on the side of reform and progress. His views on many issues seem so timeless that we can still identify with them — on the overkill of taxation, for instance:

Taxes upon every article which enters into the mouth, or covers the back, or is placed under the foot — taxes upon everything which is pleasant to see, hear, feel, smell or taste — taxes on everything on earth, and the waters under the earth . . . The schoolboy whips his taxed top, the beardless youth manages his taxed horse, with a taxed bridle, on a taxed road — and the dying Englishman, pouring his medicine, which has paid 7 per cent, into a spoon that has paid 15 per cent, flings himself back on his chintz bed, which has paid 22 per cent, and expires into the arms of an apothecary who has paid a licence of a hundred pounds for the privilege of putting him to death.

or on the evils of colonization. Smith used India as an example:

If the Bible is universally diffused in Hindustan, what must be the astonishment of the natives to find that we are forbidden to rob, murder and steal; we who, in fifty years, have extended our empire . . . over the whole peninsula . . . and exemplified in our public conduct every crime of which human nature is capable. What matchless impudence to follow up such practice with such precepts! If we have common prudence, let us keep the gospel at home, and tell them that Machiavelli is our prophet, and the god of the Manicheans our god.

All his life Smith suffered from the realization that he was mis-understood — that his great good humor was taken for buffoo-nery and his prodigious talents undervalued:

Smug Sydney.

Lord Byron (1788-1824)

A more profligate parson I never met.

George IV (1762-1830)

The truth is that Sydney Smith is naturally coarse, and a lover of scurrilous language.

John Ward, earl of Dudley (1781-1833)

He was too much of a jack-pudding.

Henry Brougham (1778-1868) on
Sydney Smith

But since he had the delightful quality of refusing to take himself too seriously, Smith remained an eloquent, high-spirited dinner guest. More and more he was forced to deal with the duties of being a social lion:

MY DEAR DICKENS,
I accept your obliging invitation conditionally. If I am invited by any man of greater genius than yourself, or one by whose works I have been more completely interested, I will repudiate you, and dine with the more splendid phenomenon of the two.

It speaks volumes for Charles Dickens's breadth of character that he maintained warm friendships with two such different beings as Landor and Smith.

Turning down invitations was a frequent Smith problem; either from necessity:

Dear Longman, I can't accept your invitation, for my house is full of country cousins. I wish they were once removed.

or from disinclination. Opera bored him to tears:

Thy servant is threescore-and-ten years old; can he hear the sound of singing men and singing women? A Canon at the Opera! Where have you lived? In what habitations of the heathen? I thank you, shuddering; and am ever your unseducible friend.

and he had little interest in protracted popular entertainments:

Music for such a length of time (unless under sentence of a jury) I will not submit to. What pleasure is there in pleasure if quantity is not attended to as well as quality?

I never go to plays, and should not care (except for the amusement of others) if there was no theatre in the whole world; it is an art intended only for amusement, and it never amuses me.

London was Sydney's milieu — London, where he was "surrounded by a Caspian sea of soup" — although the delights of the capital carried some associated drawbacks:

He who drinks a tumbler of London water has literally in his stomach more animated beings than there are men, women and children on the face of the globe.

London had conviviality: good talk, good food, cheerful fires and lights. On one occasion, Samuel Rogers experimented at a dinner party with placing the candles high on the walls, to show off his paintings. Sydney was asked how he liked the effect:

Not at all; above there is a blaze of light, and below nothing but darkness and gnashing of teeth.

So powerful was Sydney's spell that people remembered not so much what he had said, but how much they had laughed. Mrs. Siddons, the tragedian who was so dramatic that Sydney said she stabbed the potatoes at dinner, actually went into a convulsion while dining with Smith and had to be helped from the table. Such occurrences were apparently not unusual. Fortunately some of the bon mots have survived:

Go where you will, Mrs. Grote; do what you please. I have the most perfect confidence in your indiscretion.

Harrowgate is the most heaven-forgotten country under the sun. When I saw it there were only nine mangy fir trees there; and even they all leaned away from it.

Heat, ma'am? It was so dreadful here that I found there was nothing left for it but to take off my flesh and sit in my bones.

When I first saw Brighton pavilion, I thought that St. Paul's Cathedral had come down and pupped.

The departure of the Wise Men from the East seems to have been on a more extensive scale than is generally supposed, for no one of that description seems to have been left behind.

Smith's many life-long friendships withstood a constant barrage of gibes. Totally devoid of malice, these quips were nonetheless frequently wicked. Samuel Rogers had pretensions to being a poet:

Rogers is not very well. . . . Don't you know he has produced a couplet? When he is delivered of a couplet, with infinite labour and pain, he takes to his bed, has straw laid down, the knocker tied up, expects his friends to call and make enquiries, and the answer at the door invariably is "Mr. Rogers and his little couplet are as well as can be expected." When he produces an Alexandrine he keeps to his bed a day longer.
On Samuel Rogers

Sydney punctured the scholarly pretensions of one of the few bishops with whom he was on amiable terms:

I have written to Maltby ... that you have peculiar opinions
about the preterpluperfect tense; and this, I know, will bring
him directly, for that tense has always occasioned him much
uneasiness, though he has appeared to the world cheerful and
serene.

On Bishop Maltby

and made constant fun of the gourmet propensities of Henry
Luttrell:

Mr. Luttrell is going gently down-hill, trusting that the cookery
in another planet may be at least as good as in this; but not
without apprehensions that for misconduct here he may be
sentenced to a thousand years of tough mutton, or condemned
to a little eternity of family dinners.

On Henry Luttrell

Cobbett's bête noire, Malthus, who advocated population control,
was a frequent visitor:

Philosopher Malthus came here last week. I got an agreeable
party for him of unmarried people. There was only one lady
who had a child; but he is a good-natured man, and if there
are no appearances of approaching fertility, is civil to every
lady.

On Thomas Robert Malthus

Sydney greatly admired Thomas Macaulay, considering him one
of the best minds in the country. Still, this did not deter him from
endless jokes about Macaulay's tendency to non-stop talking:

I wish I could write like you. I could write an Inferno, *and I*
would put Macaulay amongst a number of disputants and
gag him.

*I spent a horrid, horrid night! I dreamt I was chained to a rock
and being talked to death by Harriet Martineau and Macaulay.*
                                    On Thomas Babington Macaulay

The devious and egotistical Henry Brougham was one of the
Review's cofounders; Smith's enthusiasm for him waned with the
years. Seeing him ride by in the strange crested carriage to which
he gave his name, Sydney remarked·

There goes a carriage with a B outside and a wasp within.
                                    On Henry Brougham

Assessing a Brougham article for the *Review*, Smith allowed that

It is long yet vigorous, like the penis of a jackass.

As he grew older, Sydney consoled himself with thoughts of
another and better world:

*We shall meet again in another planet, cured of all our defects.
Rogers will be less irritable; Macaulay more silent; Hallam will
assent; Jeffrey will speak slower; Bobus will be just as he is; and
I shall be more respectful to the upper clergy.*
                                    Sydney Smith (1771-1845)

Somehow, one rather doubts it.

CHAPTER FOUR

Of Graves, of Worms, and Epitaphs

Let's talk of graves, of worms, and epitaphs.
William Shakespeare (1564-1616) *Richard II*

In lapidary inscriptions a man is not upon oath.
Samuel Johnson (1709-1784)

Wm. SHAKESPEARE

De mortuis nihil nisi bonum — Speak nothing but good of the dead. One of mankind's oldest taboos, and still one of its most faithfully observed. And it has never been enough merely to speak no evil. A plain statement of facts, let alone a touch of irreverence, is regarded as a shocking and insulting liberty. Cynics, of course, have always taken a rather skeptical view of the fulsome obituary that celebrates the virtues and glosses over the defects of the departed:

> *Friend, in your epitaph I'm grieved*
> *So very much is said:*
> *One-half will never be believed.*
> *The other never read.*
>
> Anonymous

and have devised pointed little aphorisms to express their disenchantment:

> EPITAPH: *An inscription on a tomb, showing that virtues acquired by death have a retroactive effect.*
>
> Ambrose Bierce (1842-1914)

> *Epitaph: A belated advertisement for a line of goods that has been permanently discontinued.*
>
> Irvin S. Cobb (1876-1944)

But the taboo is a strong one. Our own age, having replaced sex with death as the ultimate obscenity, continues to toe the line. Still, there have always been squads of largely anonymous bad-mouths who delight in shocking their fellows by speaking, if not evil, at least no good of their deceased contemporaries. And most of us, with a slightly guilty relish, are only too happy to listen.

Speaking ill of the dead has sometimes involved other perils as well. As late as 1824 libel suits and imprisonment were all too real prospects. But this danger was laid to rest later in the century when a prominent Cardiff merchant went to his dubious reward. A critical solicitor of the town suggested a fitting inscription for the inevitable statue:

> *In honour of John Batchelor, a native of Newport, who in early life left his country for his country's good; who on his return devoted his life and energies to setting class against class, a traitor to the Crown, a reviler of the aristocracy, a hater of the clergy, a panderer to the multitude; who as first chairman of the Cardiff School Board, squandered funds to which he did not contribute; who is sincerely mourned by unpaid creditors to the amount of £50,000; who at the close of a wasted and misspent life died a pauper, this monument, to the eternal disgrace of Cardiff, is erected by sympathetic Radicals.*
>
> OWE NO MAN ANYTHING.
>
> Anonymous; suggested epitaph 1887

Mr. Batchelor's pained relations promptly sued for libel, but the case was lost, and the principle firmly established that one cannot libel the dead.

There were those who had never doubted it. Often the easiest way to malign the dead involved sticking strictly to the facts:

> *Here lies the body of Richard Hind,*
> *Who was neither ingenious, sober, nor kind.*
>
> Anonymous; *Webb's Epitaphs* 1775

with sometimes a little editorial comment thrown in:

> *Here Lies*
> *Ezekial Aikle*
> *Aged 102*
> *The Good*
> *Die Young*
>
> Anonymous; East Dalhousie, N.S.

A well-known atheist was determined to perpetuate his opinions from his own tombstone:

Haine Haint
                    Arthur Haine; Vancouver, B.C., cemetery

while a London journalist, succinct and to the point, managed to evaluate his friend's life in three words:

Hotten
Rotten
Forgotten
            George Augustus Henry Sala on John Camden Hotten

At first glance the composer of this epitaph seems to have been unreasonably critical —

Lord, she is Thin
                    Anonymous; Annapolis County, N.S., graveyard

but a closer look reveals that some latter-day proofreader has supplied the final *e* inadvertently omitted by the carver.

The necessity to find praiseworthy qualities where few exist has proved too much of a strain for some, who resort to indiscriminate name-dropping and damning with faint praise:

Here lies the body of
Lady O'Looney,
Great-niece of Burke, commonly
called the Sublime.
She was
Bland, passionate and deeply religious;
Also she painted in water colours,
And sent several pictures to the Exhibition.

She was first cousin to Lady Jones,
And of such is the Kingdom of Heaven.
Anonymous; Pewsey, Bedfordshire

The dead have occasionally seemed to adopt a faintly hectoring
tone toward the Almighty:

Here lie I, Martin Elginbrodde.
Ha' mercy o' my soul, Lord Godde,
As I would do were I Lord Godde,
And thou wert Martin Elginbrodde.
Anonymous

while even when a royal prince bit the dust, some observers
were unable to work up much spurious loyalty:

Here lies Fred,
Who was alive and is dead:
Had it been his father,
I had much rather;
Had it been his brother,
Still better than another;
Had it been his sister,
No one would have missed her;
Had it been the whole generation,
Still better for the nation:
But since 'tis only Fred,
Who was alive and is dead, —
There's no more to be said.
Anonymous; quoted by Horace Walpole on Frederick,
prince of Wales and the House of Hanover 1751

The same sense of ennui has been expressed by others:

Tom Smith is dead, and here he lies,
Nobody laughs and nobody cries;

Where his soul's gone, or how it fares,
Nobody knows, and nobody cares.

Anonymous; Newbury, England 1742

Naturally enough, stronger personalities evoke less indifferent views on their fate in the hereafter. At times the deceased is given the benefit of the doubt—

Here lie the bones of Robert Lowe:
Where he's gone to I don't know.
If the realms of peace and love,
Farewell to happiness above.
If he's gone to a lower level,
I can't congratulate the Devil.

E. Knatchbull-Hugessen on
Robert Lowe

Here Holy Willie's sair-worn clay
Taks up its last abode;
His saul has ta'n some other way—
I fear the left-hand road.

Robert Burns (1759-1796)

but just as often his fate is not left open to question:

> *Here lie Willie Michie's banes;*
> *O Satan, when ye tak him,*
> *Gie him the schoolin' o' your weans,*
> *For clever deils he'll mak' em!*
>
> Robert Burns (1759-1796) on a
> schoolmaster in Cleish Parish,
> Kinross-shire

> *Here lies the body of Bob Dent;*
> *He kicked up his heels and to Hell he went.*
>
> Anonymous; Grand Gulf
> Cemetery, near Port Gibson,
> Miss.

> *If heav'n be pleas'd when sinners cease to sin,*
> *If hell be pleas'd when souls are damn'd therein,*
> *If earth be pleas'd when it's rid of a knave,*
> *Then all are pleas'd, for Coleman's in his grave.*
>
> Anonymous, 1704

In extreme cases, even the demons are not happy to receive one of their own:

> *When X deceased and passed below,*
> *Earth jumped for joy. "For you 'tis well,"*
> *Said Nick, "but I should like to know*
> *Why was this monster sent to Hell?"*
>
> F. P. Barnard

The foibles of the well-born, the famous and the infamous are particularly likely to be commemorated in less than complimentary terms. This happy play on words records the passing of a tactfully unnamed scion of the aristocracy who had committed a heinous social sin:

Here lies
Henry William, twenty-second Lord ————,
In Joyful expectation of the last trump.

Lord Alvanley (1745-1804) on a
noble lord who had been
expelled from society for
cheating at whist

Those who had held unpopular opinions could provoke violent reactions:

Died in Vermont the profane and
impious Deist Gen. Ethan Allen. . . .
And in Hell he lift up his eyes, being in
Torments.

Ezra Stiles (1727-1795) on Ethan Allen 1789

But even notorious wrongdoers sometimes prompted a more ambiguous response. The dashing criminal always seems to inspire a sneaking admiration:

Here lies DuVall; reader if male thou art,
Look to thy purse; if female to thy heart.

Anonymous; Covent Garden
Church; on highwayman Claude
DuVall

Although strictly speaking he was not a criminal, an innovative minister of Louis XIV probably fared better than he deserved. Sydney Smith might have approved:

Here lies the father of taxation:
May Heaven, his faults forgiving,
Grant him repose; which he, while living,
Would never grant the nation.

R. A. Davenport (1777-1852) on Jean Baptiste Colbert

Even the longest and noblest lineage, apparently, is no guarantee against a sticky end:

Bright ran thy line, O Galloway,
Thro' many a far-fam'd sire;
So ran the far-fam'd Roman way,
So ended in a mire!
Robert Burns (1759-1796) on Lord Galloway

The spiteful and malicious denizens of the artistic world have naturally enough supplied a wealth of material for lapidary philosophers. A well-known comic actor met an appropriate end:

Foote from his earthly stage, alas! is hurl'd;
Death took him off, who took off all the world.
Anonymous; Dodd's Select
Epigrams 1797; on Samuel Foote

Artistic feuds are frequently carried beyond the grave. A brilliant but erratic poet could not let the leading painter of his day rest in peace:

O reader behold the philosopher's grave!
He was born quite a fool but he died quite a knave.
William Blake (1757-1827) on Sir Joshua Reynolds

while a critic who had produced a bad-tempered and vindictive epitaph on Samuel Johnson became, in turn, the victim of a nasty little rebuke:

Here lies a little ugly nauseous elf,
Who judging only from its wretched self,
Feebly attempted, petulant and vain,
The 'Origin of Evil' to explain.
Anonymous; on Soame Jenyns

Every so often the epitaph is used to poke fun at society. The poet Samuel Butler received meager financial rewards during his lifetime, but a monument was erected to him on his death:

> *Whilst Butler, needy wretch! was yet alive,*
> *No gen'rous patron would a dinner give:*
> *See him when starved to death, and turn'd to dust,*
> *Presented with a monumental bust!*
> *The poet's fate is here in emblem shown, —*
> *He ask'd for bread, and he receiv'd a stone.*
>
> Samuel Wesley (1810-1876) on
> Samuel Butler

Would-be poets, too, may find that lack of appreciation lingers after them:

> *Here lies that peerless paper peer Lord Peter,*
> *Who broke the laws of God and man and metre.*
>
> Sir Walter Scott (1771-1832) on
> Patrick ("Peter") Lord Robertson

and the enemies of some authors pen acrimonious but premature epitaphs in undisguised anticipation. G. K. Chesterton had a tendency to pontificate:

> *Poor G.K.C., his day is past —*
> *Now God will know the truth at last.*
>
> E. V. Lucas (1868-1938) on G. K.
> Chesterton; proposed epitaph

and his critics perceived an unpleasant streak of anti-Semitism in his views:

> *Here lies Mr. Chesterton,*
> *who to heaven might have gone,*
> *But didn't when he heard the news*
> *That the place was run by Jews.*
>
> Humbert Wolfe (1886-1940) on
> G. K. Chesterton; proposed epitaph

Nor have the discoveries of science always been welcome with open arms. Alexander Pope had celebrated the theories of Newton in a famous couplet:

> *Nature and Nature's law, lay hid in night:*
> *God said,* Let Newton be! *and all was light.*
> Alexander Pope (1688-1744)

but a modern observer, contemplating the upheaval in scientific thought, penned a sardonic reply:

> *It did not last: the Devil, howling* Ho!
> Let Einstein be! *restored the status quo.*
> J. C. Squire (1884-1958) on
Albert Einstein

EINSTEIN

In one fantasy at least, the esoteric mathematician became the victim of his own speculations on the uncertainties of modern life:

> *Here Einstein lies;*
> *At least, they laid his bier*
> *Just hereabouts —*
> *Or relatively near.*
>
> Kensal Green on Albert Einstein

The epitaph has provided countless fond husbands a last chance to express the true depth of marital devotion —

> *I laid my wife*
> *Beneath this stone,*
> *For her repose*
> *And for my own.*
>
> Anonymous; Ottawa graveyard

> *Here lies my wife,*
> *Here lies she;*
> *Hallelujah!*
> *Hallelujee!*
>
> Anonymous; Leeds graveyard; *Norfolk's Epitaphs* 1861

— feelings shared by a great English poet:

> *Here lies my wife: here let her lie!*
> *Now she's at rest, and so am I.*
>
> John Dryden (1631-1700) on his wife

A few short lines can be enough to portray the gripping and sometimes tragic drama of domestic life:

Papa loved mamma
Mamma loved men
Mamma's in the graveyard
Papa's in the pen

Carl Sandburg (1878-1967)

while the burdens of family decision-making are evident even in the graveyard:

Here lies the mother of children seven,
Four on earth and three in heaven;
The three in heaven preferring rather
To die with mother than live with father.

Anonymous; Birmingham graveyard

For some people, the most noteworthy thing in life is their manner of leaving it:

Here lies John Tyrwitt
A learned divine;
He died in a fit
Through drinking port wine
Died 3rd April, 1828, aged 59

Anonymous; Malta 1828

Against his will
Here lies George Hill,
Who from a cliff
Fell down quite stiff.
When it happen'd is not known,
Therefore not mentioned on this stone.

Anonymous; St. Peter's
Churchyard, Isle of Thanet

To the Memory
of
Abraham Beaulieu
Born 15 September
1822
Accidentally shot
4th April 1844
As a mark of affection
from his brother

Anonymous

Nothing in this melancholy chapter of accidents, however, can be quite so affecting as this cautionary tale:

In memory of
THOMAS THATCHER,
A Grenadier of the Ninth Regiment
of Hants Militia, who died of a
violent fever, contracted by drinking
small beer when hot the 12th of May,
1769, aged 26 years. . . .
Here sleeps in peace a Hampshire Grenadier
Who caught his death by drinking cold small beer.
Soldiers, be wise from his untimely fall,
And when ye're hot, drink strong or none at all.

Anonymous; Winchester
Cathedral yard

Given the obvious perils of living, it would seem that this plaintive child did not know when he was well off:

It is so soon that I am done for,
I wonder what I was begun for.

Anonymous; child's grave, Cheltenham

The ultimate form of accident insurance appears to have been adopted by a provident Oxfordshire gentleman who clearly believed in taking no chances:

> *Here lies the body of John Eldred.*
> *At least he will be here when he is dead;*
> *But now at this time he is alive*
> *The 14th August, Sixty Five.*
>
> John Eldred; Oxfordshire churchyard 1765

Of all men, politicians are the most open to scorn and ridicule — and it often follows them to the grave. The species as a whole tends to be distinctly unappreciated:

> *There lies beneath this mossy stone*
> *A politician who*
> *Touched a live issue without gloves,*
> *And never did come to.*
>
> Keith Preston

Even obscure politicians find their less attractive qualities under attack. This one was always in too much of a hurry:

> *Lay aside, all yet dead,*
> *For in the next bed*
> *Reposes the body of Cushing;*
> *He has crowded his way*
> *Through the world, as they say,*
> *And even though dead will keep pushing.*
>
> Hanna F. Gould on Caleb Cushing; proposed epitaph

and some invite even stronger disapprobation. Lord Byron loathed Viscount Castlereagh, but with misdirected nineteenth-century delicacy required the reader to supply the missing rhyme:

Posterity will ne'er survey
A nobler grave than this;
Here lies the bones of Castlereagh:
Stop traveller, —— ——

Lord Byron (1788-1824)

LORD
BYRON

A long-time member of the British House of Commons summarized the general attitude toward politicians:

Here richly, with ridiculous display,
The Politician's corpse was laid away.
While all of his acquaintance sneered and slanged,
I wept: for I had longed to see him hanged.

Hilaire Belloc (1870-1953)

Politics was not the only profession to attract the creators of tombstone literature. The matching of the deceased's occupation to an apt inscription became something of a folk art. Few practitioners were as blatant as this enterprising husband:

Here lies Jane Smith, wife of Thomas Smith, marble cutter. This monument was erected by her husband as a tribute to her memory and a specimen of his work. Monuments of the same style 350 dollars.

Thomas Smith

but the architect of Blenheim Palace was the victim of a suitably heavy-handed figure of speech:

Under this stone, Reader, survey
Dead Sir John Vanbrugh's house of clay.
Lie heavy on him, Earth! for he
Laid many heavy loads on thee!

Abel Evans (1679-1737) on Sir
John Vanbrugh

Not many prophecies have been as grotesque as this one about a lady who ran a pottery shop:

Beneath this stone lies Catherine Gray,
Changed to a lifeless lump of clay.
By earth and clay she got her pelf,
And now she's turned to earth herself.
Ye weeping friends let me advise,
Abate your tears and dry your eyes;
For what avails a flood of tears?
Who knows but in a course of years,
In some tall pitcher or brown pan,
She in her shop may be again?

Anonymous; in a Chester, England, church

The ever-waspish Byron could not resist this observation on the fate of a toping carrier:

> *John Adams lies here, of the parish of Southwell,*
> *A Carrier who carried his can to his mouth well:*
> *He carried so much, and he carried so fast,*
> *He could carry no more — so was carried at last;*
> *For the liquor he drank, being too much for one,*
> *He could not carry off, — so he's now carrion.*
>
> Lord Byron (1788-1824) on John Adams

and another commentator pointed out the evil effects of social climbing on a weaver who would not stick to his loom:

> *Geta from wool and weaving first began*
> *Swelling and swelling to a Gentleman;*
> *When he was Gentleman and bravely dight,*
> *He left not swelling till he was a knight:*
> *At last (forgetting what he was at first)*
> *He swole to be a Lord, and then he burst.*
>
> Thomas Bastard (1566-1618)

Certain occupations seemed heaven-sent for a satirical dig:

> *A zealous locksmith died of late,*
> *And did arrive at Heaven's gate.*
> *He stood without, and would not knock,*
> *Because he meant to pick the lock.*
>
> Anonymous; *Camden's Remains* 1623

including that favorite target, the money-lender:

> *Here lies old twenty-five percent,*
> *The more he had, the more he lent.*

The more he had, the more he craved,
Great God, can this poor soul be saved?

Anonymous; Nova Scotia 19th century

As popular as a gloss on occupations was a play on names. Generations of epitaph-makers have been unable to resist a pun:

"Fuller's earth."

Thomas Fuller (1608-1661) on himself

Urn a lively Hood.

Thomas Hood (1835-1874) on himself

Alack, and well-a-day,
Potter himself is turned to clay¹

Anonymous; on Archbishop
Potter 1747

Here lies a Bond under this tomb
Seal'd and deliver'd to God knows whom.

Anonymous; *Wit Restored* 1658;
on Bond the Usurer

Some authors tried a little harder, and produced more ambitious images:

When from the chrysalis of the tomb
I rise in rainbow-colour'd plume,
My weeping friends, ye scarce will know
That I was but a Grubb below.

Anonymous; *Booth's Epitaphs*
1868; on John Grubb

Under this sod
And under these trees
Lieth the body of Solomon Pease.

He's not in this hole,
But only his pod;
He shelled out his soul
And went up to God.

Anonymous; Ohio tombstone

What! kill a partridge in the month of May!
Was that done like a sportsman? Eh, Death, eh?

Anonymous; Norfolk's Epitaphs
1861; on Mr. Partridge

But there is no question that the energies of some authors have been totally misapplied. Words cannot describe the pedantic wag who is addicted to the Latin pun:

Ars longa, vita brevis.

Anonymous; on Thomas Longbottom

The play on words has always been popular in epitaphs:

These walls, so full of monument and bust,
Show how Bath waters serve to lay the dust.

Henry Harington, M.D.; Abbey
Church, Bath

This line of thought, pursued to its extreme, results in the avowedly comic epitaph. One of these maligns Cobbett's favorite resort:

Here lie I and my four daughters,
Killed by drinking Cheltenham waters.
Had we but stuck to Epsom salts,
We wouldn't have been in these here vaults.

Anonymous; Norfolk's Epitaphs 1861

while another attests to the strength and endurance of family affection:

> *Beneath this stone, in hopes of Zion,*
> *Doth lie the landlord of the Lion;*
> *His son keeps on the business still,*
> *Resigned unto the heavenly will.*
>
> Anonymous; *Fairley's*
> *Epitaphiana* 1875; on an
> innkeeper

and yet another comments on persistence in the face of apparently overwhelming odds:

> *Here lies all that remains of Charlotte,*
> *Born a virgin, died a harlot.*
> *For sixteen years she kept her virginity,*
> *A marvellous thing for this vicinity.*
>
> Anonymous; Welland, Ont.

Today's liberated women would no doubt deplore the conditions described by this oppressed sister — but one wonders if they are entirely obsolete:

> *Here lies a poor woman who always was tired;*
> *She lived in a house where help was not hired.*
> *Her last words on earth were: "Dear friends, I am going*
> *Where washing ain't done, nor sweeping, nor sewing:*
> *But everything there is exact to my wishes;*
> *For where they don't eat there's no washing of dishes. . . .*
> *Don't mourn for me now; don't mourn for me never —*
> *I'm going to do nothing for ever and ever."*
>
> Anonymous; *The Tired Woman's Epitaph*

One way of striking back at the epitaph-maker is to write one's own. Tradition has it that the Bard himself composed his memorial, although the quality of the verse speaks against it:

> *Good friend for Jesus sake, forebaere,*
> *To dig the dust encloased heare*
> *Blest be ye man yt spares thes stones,*
> *And curst be he yt moves my bones.*
>
> Shakespeare's epitaph; Stratford-on-Avon

Many intrepid souls have commended their own best qualities to posterity:

> *When I am dead, I hope it may be said:*
> *"His sins were scarlet but his books were read."*
>
> Hilaire Belloc (1870-1953)

> *He reads but he cannot speak Spanish,*
> *He cannot abide ginger beer:*
> *Ere the days of his pilgrimage vanish,*
> *How pleasant to know Mr. Lear!*
>
> Edward Lear (1812-1888)

A faintly self-deprecatory air is considered de rigueur:

> *Here lies one who meant well, tried a little, failed much*
>
> Robert Louis Stevenson (1850-1894)

although few have had such good reason for self-criticism as the emperor Joseph:

> *Let my epitaph be, "Here lies Joseph, who failed in everything he undertook."*
>
> Joseph II, Holy Roman Emperor 1790

The contemplation of a better world did not seem to alarm H. L. Mencken:

> *If, after I depart this vale, you remember me and have some thought to please my ghost, forgive some sinner and wink your eye at a homely girl.*
>
> H. L. Mencken (1880-1956)

But perhaps the most profound comment on the hereafter was expressed by a notable curmudgeon:

> *On the whole, I'd rather be in Philadelphia.*
>
> W. C. Fields (1880-1946)

While the frivolous epitaph has its place, the glory of the art undoubtedly lies in the full-blown, carefully constructed, total condemnation of one's fellow man. Few examples can match this balanced and reasoned eighteenth-century excoriation of a thoroughgoing villain:

> HERE *continueth to rot*
> *The Body of* FRANCIS CHARTRES,
> *Who with inflexible constancy,*
> *and Inimitable Uniformity of Life*
> *Persisted*
> *In spite of Age and Infirmities*
> *In the practice of Every Human Vice;*
> *Excepting Prodigality and Hypocrisy:*
> *His insatiable Avarice exempted him from the first,*
> *His matchless Impudence from the second.*
> *Nor was he more singular*
> *in the undeviating Pravity of his Manners*
> *Than successful*
> *In Accumulating* WEALTH . . .

He was the only Person of his Time
Who cou'd cheat without the Mask of Honesty
Retain his Primeval Meanness
When possess'd of Ten Thousand a Year
And having daily deserved the Gibbet for what he did,
Was at last condemn'd to it for what he could not do.
> Dr. John Arbuthnot (1667-1735)
> on Francis Chartres, gambler,
> brothel-keeper, money-lender

Only the most impenitent of sinners would not feel the sting of such a posthumous indictment. But occasionally a counteroffensive is launched from beyond the grave. The final will and testament has provided a golden opportunity for some hardy individualists to have, truly, the last word.

A goodly number of those who were about to die apparently set about it in a distinctly uncharitable mood, nursing to the end their grievances against their nearest and dearest. One Samuel Baldwin was buried at sea in 1736; in choosing this mode of interment he managed to score off his wife one final time, Mrs. Baldwin having promised to dance on his grave if she survived him. The settling of marital accounts shows a record of continually diminishing returns:

I give to Elizabeth Parker the sum of £50, whom, through my foolish fondness, I made my wife; and who in return has not spared, most unjustly, to accuse me of every crime regarding human nature, save highway-robbery.
> Charles Parker, 1785

I do give and bequeath to Mary Davis the sum of five shillings, which is sufficient to enable her to get drunk for the last time at my expense.
> David Davis, 1788

I give unto my wife Mary Darley, for picking my pocket of 60 guineas, and taking up money in my name, the sum of one shilling.

William Darley, 1794

The serpent's tooth of filial ingratitude has stung many a father. Some have struck back:

To my only son, who never would follow my advice, and has treated me rudely in many circumstances, I give him nothing.

Richard Crashaw, 1810

But one noble and inventive parent left his wayward boy a particularly grisly memorial:

I leave my right hand, to be cut off after my death, to my son Lord Audley; in hopes that such a sight may remind him of his duty to God, after having so long abandoned the duty he owed to a father who once affectionately loved him.

Philip Thicknesse, 1793

The effect of this kind remembrance on young Audley has not been recorded.

The eccentric William "Tiger" Dunlop was a prominent figure in the settlement of Ontario, and gathered around him a large family. The temptation to take posthumous potshots at his loved ones proved too much for him, as witness his famous last will and testament:

In the name of God. Amen.
I, William Dunlop, of Gairbraid, in the Township of Colborne, County and District of Huron, Western Canada, Esquire, being in sound health of body, and my mind just as

*usual (which my friends who flatter me say is no great shakes
at the best of times), do make this my last Will and Testament
as follows, revoking, of course, all former Wills:*

*I leave the property of Gairbraid, and all other landed prop-
erty I may die possessed of, to my sisters Helen Boyle Story and
Elizabeth Boyle Dunlop; the former because she is married to
a minister whom (God help him) she henpecks. The latter because she is married to nobody, nor is she like to be, for she
is an old maid, and not market-rife. . . .*

*I leave my silver tankard to the eldest son of old John, as
the representative of the family. I would have left it to old John
himself, but he would melt it down to make temperance med-
als, and that would be sacrilege — however, I leave my big
horn snuffbox to him; he can only make temperance horn
spoons out of that. . . .*

*I also leave my late brother's watch to my brother Sandy,
exhorting him at the same time to give up Whiggery, Radical-
ism, and all other sins that do most easily beset him. . . .*

*I leave Parson Chevasse (Magg's husband), the snuff-box I
got from the Sarnia Militia, as a small token of my gratitude
for the service he has done the family in taking a sister that no
man of taste would have taken.*

*I leave John Caddle a silver teapot, to the end that he may
drink tea therefrom to comfort him under the affliction of a
slatternly wife.*

*I leave my books to my brother Andrew, because he has been
so long a Jungley Wallah, that he may learn to read with
them. . . .*

*In witness whereof I have hereunto set my hand and seal
the thirty-first day of August, in the year of our Lord one thousand eight hundred and forty-two.*

W. DUNLOP

William Dunlop (1792-1848)

Tiger Dunlop must have died a happy man. What better ending for a true curmudgeon than to have the last word — an unkind one?

> *Here lies Aretino, Tuscan poet*
> *Who spoke evil of everyone but God,*
> *Giving the excuse, "I never knew Him."*
>
> Anonymous

Index of Authors

Index of Subjects